The Fran Lebowitz Reader

Fran Lebowitz still lives in New York City, as she does not believe that she would be allowed to live anywhere else.

Books by

Fran Lebowitz

The
Fran
Lebowitz
Reader

The Fran Lebowitz Reader

Vintage Books

A Division of Random House, Inc.

New York

FIRST VINTAGE BOOKS EDITION, NOVEMBER 1994

Some of these pieces appeared originally in Andy Warhol's
Interview and in *Mademoiselle*. "MY DAY: An Introduction of
Sorts" appeared in British *Vogue* in a slightly different form.

ISBN: 0-679-76180-2
Library of Congress Catalog Card Number: 94-61671

Manufactured in the United States of America
56789B

for Lisa Robinson

Contents

SCIENCE

ARTS

LETTERS

SOCIAL STUDIES

IDEAS

Preface

The first of the pieces in this volume were written in my early twenties — the last, in my early thirties. I am now in what only the most partisan and utopian of observers would describe as my early forties. It is therefore unsurprising that the question of what used to be called relevance (exactly) has been raised. Allow me then, to lower it.

Although it is true that mood rings, CB radio, disco, high-tech interior decoration, and safe sex with strangers are either no longer novel or extant, it cannot be denied that many such things (although not, alas, the last) have been frequently revived, and that in this singularly dull and retroactive era to require timeliness of a writer, when it is no longer even required of timeliness, is not only grossly unfair, but also unseemly.

If what is presently called art can be called art, and what is presently called history can be called history (indeed, if what is presently called the present can be called the present), then I urge the contemporary reader — that solitary figure — to accept these writings in the spirit in which they were originally intended and are once again offered: as art history. But art history with a difference; modern, pertinent, current, up-to-the-minute art history. Art history in the making.

Fran Lebowitz
September 1994

Metropolitan Life

My Day:
An Introduction of Sorts

12:35 P.M.—The phone rings. I am not amused. This is not my favorite way to wake up. My favorite way to wake up is to have a certain French movie star whisper to me softly at two-thirty in the afternoon that if I want to get to Sweden in time to pick up my Nobel Prize for Literature I had better ring for breakfast. This occurs rather less often than one might wish.

Today is a perfect example, for my caller is an agent from Los Angeles who informs me that I don't know him. True, and not without reason. He is audibly tan. He is interested in my work. His interest has led him to the conclusion that it would be a good idea for me to write a movie comedy. I would, of course, have total artistic freedom, for evidently comic writers have taken over the movie business. I look around my apartment (a feat readily accomplished by simply glancing up) and remark that Dino De Laurentiis would be surprised to hear that. He chuckles tanly and suggests that we talk. I suggest that we *are* talking. He, however, means *there* and at my own expense. I reply that the only way I could get to Los Angeles at my own expense is if I were to go by postcard. He chuckles again and suggests that we talk. I agree to talk just as soon as I have won the Nobel Prize—for outstanding achievement in physics.

12:55 P.M.—I try to get back to sleep. Although sleeping is an area in which I have manifested an almost Algeresque grit and persistence, I fail to attain my goal.

1:20 P.M.—I go downstairs to get the mail. I get back into bed. Nine press releases, four screening notices, two bills, an invitation to a party in honor of a celebrated heroin addict, a final disconnect notice from New York Telephone, and three hate letters from *Mademoiselle* readers demanding to know just what it is that makes me think that I have the right to regard houseplants—*green, living* things—with such marked distaste. I call the phone company and try to make a deal, as actual payment is not a possibility. Would they like to go to a screening? Would they care to attend a party for a heroin addict? Are they interested in knowing just what it is that makes me think that I have the right to regard houseplants with such marked distaste? It seems they would not. They would like $148.10. I agree that this is, indeed, an understandable preference, but caution them against the bloodless quality of a life devoted to the blind pursuit of money. We are unable to reach a settlement. I pull up the covers and the phone rings. I spend the next few hours fending off editors, chatting amiably, and plotting revenge. I read. I smoke. The clock, unfortunately, catches my eye.

3:40 P.M.—I consider getting out of bed. I reject the notion as being unduly vigorous. I read and smoke a bit more.

4:15 P.M.—I get up feeling curiously unrefreshed. I open the refrigerator. I decide against the half a lemon and jar of Gulden's mustard and on the spur of the moment choose instead to have breakfast out. I guess that's just the kind of girl I am—whimsical.

5:10 P.M.—I return to my apartment laden with magazines and spend the remainder of the afternoon reading articles by writers who, regrettably, met their deadlines.

6:55 P.M.—A romantic interlude. The object of my affections arrives bearing a houseplant.

9:30 P.M.—I go to dinner with a group of people that includes two fashion models, a fashion photographer, a fashion photographer's representative, and an art director. I occupy myself almost entirely with the art director —drawn to him largely because he knows the most words.

2:05 A.M.—I enter my apartment and prepare to work. In deference to the slight chill I don two sweaters and an extra pair of socks. I pour myself a club soda and move the lamp next to the desk. I reread several old issues of *Rona Barrett's Hollywood* and a fair piece of *The Letters of Oscar Wilde*. I pick up my pen and stare at the paper. I light a cigarette. I stare at the paper. I write, "My Day: An Introduction of Sorts." Good. Lean yet cadenced. I consider my day. I become unaccountably depressed. I doodle in the margin. I jot down an idea I have for an all-black version of a Shakespearean comedy to be called *As You Likes It*. I look longingly at my sofa, not unmindful of the fact that it converts cleverly into a bed. I light a cigarette. I stare at the paper.

4:50 A.M.—The sofa wins. Another victory for furniture.

Manners

Manners

I am not a callous sort. I believe that all people should have warm clothing, sufficient food, and adequate shelter. I do feel, however, that unless they are willing to behave in an acceptable manner they should bundle up, chow down, and stay home.

I speak here not only of etiquette, for while etiquette is surely a factor, acceptable behavior is comprised of a good deal more. It demands, for instance, that the general public refrain from starting trends, overcoming inhibitions, or developing hidden talents. It further requires acceptance of the fact that the common good is usually not very and that there is indeed such a thing as getting carried away with democracy. Oppression and/or repression are not without their charms nor freedom and/or license their drawbacks. This can clearly be seen in the following chart.

THE BY-PRODUCTS OF OPPRES-SION AND/OR REPRESSION	THE BY-PRODUCTS OF FREEDOM AND/OR LICENSE

WOMEN

1. Well-kept fingernails	1. The word *chairperson*
2. Homemade cookies	2. The acceptance of construction boots as suitable attire for members of the fair sex
3. A guarantee that at least one segment of the population could be relied upon to display a marked distaste for strenuous physical activity	3. Girl ministers
4. The distinct probability that even a small gathering would yield at least one person who knew how to respond properly to a wedding invitation	4. The male centerfold
5. Real coffee	5. Erica Jong

JEWS

1. Highly entertaining stand-up comedians	1. Progressive nursery schools
2. The Stage Delicatessen	2. Frozen bagels
3. A guarantee that at least one segment of the population could be relied upon to display a marked distaste for strenuous physical activity	3. The Upper West Side

4. The development and perfection of theatrical law as a flourishing profession

4. The notion that it is appropriate for a writer to surrender a percentage of his income to an agent

5. Interesting slang expressions, particularly those used to describe Gentiles

5. Erica Jong

BLACKS

1. Jazz

1. Strawberry wine

2. The provision of the southern portion of the United States with a topic of conversation

2. Negro accountants

3. Tap dancing

3. Inventive forms of handshaking

4. The preservation in our culture of a lively interest in revenge

4. Open admissions

5. Amos 'n' Andy

5. Sammy Davis, Jr.

6. Interesting slang expressions, particularly those used to describe white people

6. The Symbionese Liberation Army

TEEN-AGERS

1. The thrill of illicit drinking

1. Strawberry wine

2. Sexual denial and the resultant development of truly exciting sexual fantasies

2. Easy sexual access and the resultant premature boredom

3. The swank of juvenile delinquency

3. Social commitment

4. The glamour of alienation

4. People who may very well just be discovering symbolist poetry being allowed to vote

HOMOSEXUALS

1. Precision theatrical dancing

1. *A Chorus Line*

2. Sarcasm

2. Amyl nitrate

3. Art

3. Leather underwear

4. Literature

4. Lesbian mothers

5. Real gossip

5. Heterosexual hairdressers

6. The amusing notion that *Who's Afraid of Virginia Woolf* was really about two men

6. The amusing notion that *Who's Afraid of Virginia Woolf* was really about a man and a woman

Two basic steps must be taken in order to reach the eventual goal of acceptable behavior. The first (which I assume you have already accomplished) is a careful perusal of the above chart. The second is ridding oneself of certain popular and harmful misconceptions, as follows:

It is not true that there is dignity in all work. Some jobs are definitely better than others. It is not hard to tell the good jobs from the bad. People who have good jobs are happy, rich, and well dressed. People who have bad jobs are unhappy, poor and use meat extenders. Those who seek dignity in the type of work that compels them to help hamburgers are certain to be disappointed. Also to be behaving badly.

There is no such thing as inner peace. There is only nervousness or death. Any attempt to prove otherwise constitutes unacceptable behavior.

Very few people possess true artistic ability. It is therefore both unseemly and unproductive to irritate the situation by making an effort. If you have a burning, restless urge to write or paint, simply eat something sweet and the feeling will pass. Your life story would not make a good book. Do not even try.

All God's children are not beautiful. Most of God's children are, in fact, barely presentable. The most common error made in matters of appearance is the belief that one should disdain the superficial and let the true beauty of one's soul shine through. If there are places on your body where this is a possibility, you are not attractive—you are leaking.

Vocational Guidance
for the Truly Ambitious

People of every age are interested in bettering themselves. It is with this in mind that the majority choose
their life work. Most professions require specific training and skills. Some, however—those a bit off the beaten
track—must be entered in a different fashion. Since
these fields are often the most difficult to gain a foothold
in, one is advised to make certain that one is really
suited to this type of work. It is with this in mind that
I offer the following series of tests.

So You Want to Be the Pope?

This position has traditionally been reserved for men.
Women interested in this job should be warned of the
almost insurmountable odds against them. Religion
also plays an important role here, so if you have your
doubts you would be well advised to consider something
a touch less restrictive.

    1. I most enjoy speaking . . .
      a. On the phone.
      b. After dinner.

   c. Off the cuff.

   d. In private.

   e. Ex cathedra.

2. Of the following, my favorite name is . . .

   a. Muffy.

   b. Vito.

   c. Ira.

   d. Jim Bob.

   e. Innocent XIII.

3. Most of my friends are . . .

   a. Left-wing intellectuals

   b. Loose women.

   c. Quality people.

   d. Regular guys.

   e. Good sports.

   f. Cardinals.

4. All roads lead to . . .

   a. Bridgehampton.

   b. Cap d'Antibes.

   c. Midtown.

   d. Tampa.

   e. Rome.

5. Complete this phrase or word. Dog . . .

   a. House.

   b. Food.

   c. Tired.

   d. Days.

   e. ma.

6. My friends call me . . .

   a. Stretch.

   b. Doc.

   c. Toni.

   d. Izzy.

   e. Supreme Pontiff.

7. For dress-up occasions I prefer . . .

   a. Something kicky yet elegant.

   b. Anything by Halston.

   c. Evening pajamas.

   d. A surplice and miter.

8. I would feel most secure knowing that I had . . .

   a. Enough money.

   b. A good alarm system.

   c. A big dog.

    d. A union contract.
    e. The Swiss Guard.
9. When annoyed at myself for taking it too easy I . . .
    a. Go on a low-carbohydrate diet.
    b. Read Emerson.
    c. Swim forty laps.
    d. Chop firewood.
    e. Wash the feet of the poor.

So You Want to Be an Heiress?

This is a field in which accident of birth carries a lot of weight. One can overcome the problem by marrying well and/or making an old man very happy. Such a method is, however, by no means easy and the lazy would do well to seek employment elsewhere.

1. If I had to describe myself in just one word, that word would be . . .
    a. Kindly.
    b. Energetic.
    c. Curious.
    d. Pleasant.
    e. Madcap.
2. I cross . . .
    a. Only after looking both ways.
    b. Town by bus.
    c. The days off the calendar.
    d. My sevens.
3. On weekends I like to go . . .
    a. Camping.
    b. Roller skating.
    c. For long walks.
    d. Bar hopping.
    e. To Gstaad.
4. I find that a good way to break the ice with people is to ask them where they . . .
    a. Buy their vegetables.
    b. Shop for appliances.
    c. Get their pictures developed.
    d. Winter.

5. Poppy is . . .
   a. A red flower.
   b. Heroin in the raw.
   c. A type of seed that appears occasionally in bread and rolls.
   d. My nickname.
6. Men make the best . . .
   a. Fried chicken.
   b. Flower arrangements.
   c. Drinks.
   d. Valets.
7. As a small child I liked to play . . .
   a. Dolls.
   b. Doctor.
   c. Baseball.
   d. Candyland.
   e. Mansion.
8. I never carry . . .
   a. A briefcase.
   b. Tales.
   c. Typhoid.
   d. Cash.
9. My first big crush was on . . .
   a. Tab Hunter.
   b. Paul McCartney.
   c. The boy next door.
   d. My horse.

So You Want to Be an Absolute Political Dictator?

This job requires stamina, drive, and an iron will. Not recommended for the shy type.

1. My greatest fear is . . .
   a. Meeting new people.
   b. Heights.
   c. Snakes.
   d. The dark.
   e. A coup d'etat.
2. On a lazy Sunday afternoon I most enjoy . . .
   a. Cooking.
   b. Experimenting with makeup.

    c. Going to a museum.

    d. Just lounging around the house.

    e. Exiling people.

3. I think people look best in . . .

    a. Formal attire.

    b. Bathing suits.

    c. Clothes that reflect their life-style.

    d. Bermuda shorts.

    e. Prison uniforms.

4. When confronted by a large crowd of strangers my immediate reaction is to . . .

    a. Introduce myself to anyone who looks interesting.

    b. Wait for them to speak to me first.

    c. Sit in a corner and sulk.

    d. Start a purge.

5. The proper manner in which to respond to a chance meeting with me is by . . .

    a. Smiling.

    b. Nodding.

    c. Saying hello.

    d. Giving me a little kiss.

    e. Saluting.

6. When someone disagrees with me my first instinct is to . . .

    a. Try to understand his point of view.

    b. Get into a pet.

    c. Discuss it calmly and rationally.

    d. Cry.

    e. Have him executed.

7. Nothing builds character like . . .

    a. Scouting.

    b. The YMCA.

    c. Sunday school.

    d. Cold showers.

    e. Forced labor.

So You Want to Be a Social Climber?

Of all the occupations dealt with here, this is undoubtedly the easiest to crack. It is also, alas, the hardest to stomach—a fact that seems to have had surprisingly little effect upon the hordes that crowd the field.

1. When alone I most often . . .
   a. Read.
   b. Watch television.
   c. Write sonnets.
   d. Build model planes.
   e. Call the Beverly Hills Hotel and have myself paged.
2. Were a female friend to say something particularly amusing I would most likely . . .
   a. Say, "Hey, that was really funny."
   b. Laugh delightedly.
   c. Giggle uncontrollably.
   d. Say, "You're so like Dottie."
3. When the phone rings I am most likely to answer by saying . . .
   a. "Hello, how are you?"
   b. "Oh, hello."
   c. "Hi."
   d. "Oh, hi, I was just listening to one of Wolfgang's little symphonies."
4. If my house or apartment was on fire the first thing I would save would be . . .
   a. My son.
   b. My cat.
   c. My boyfriend.
   d. My mention in *Women's Wear Daily*.
5. I consider dining out to be . . .
   a. A pleasure.
   b. A nice change.
   c. An opportunity to see friends.
   d. A romantic interlude.
   e. A career.
6. My idea of a good party is . . .
   a. A big, noisy bash, with lots of liquor and lots of action.
   b. Good talk, good food, good wine.
   c. A few close friends for dinner and bridge.
   d. One to which I cannot get invited.
7. If I were stranded alone on a desert island and could have only one book I would want . . .
   a. The Bible.
   b. The Complete Works of William Shakespeare.
   c. *The Wind in the Willows*.
   d. Truman Capote's address book.

8. Some of my best friends are . . .
   a. Jewish.
   b. Negro.
   c. Puerto Rican.
   d. Unaware of my existence.
9. As far as I am concerned, a rose by any other name is . . .
   a. Still the same.
   b. A flower.
   c. A color.
   d. A scent.
   e. A Kennedy.

So You Want to Be an Empress?

Once again we are confronted with the problem of family connections. Do not be deceived, however, by this job's apparent similarity to the heiress game, for it requires a good deal more responsibility. You would be a very foolish girl, though, were you to let that discourage you, for this is the only sort of work that offers the richly rewarding satisfactions of being served by others.

1. Complete the following phrase: Ladies . . .
   a. Room.
   b. Lunch.
   c. Watches.
   d. First.
   e. -in-waiting.
2. My pet peeve about my husband is his . . .
   a. Snoring.
   b. Habit of leaving the cap off the toothpaste.
   c. Drinking buddies.
   d. Stubbornness.
   e. Imperial concubines.
3. I simply don't know what I'd do without my . . .
   a. WaterPik.
   b. Answering service.
   c. Mr. Coffee.
   d. Official taster.

4. I think that the best way to get ahead in the world is by . . .
   a. Hard work.
   b. Good connections.
   c. Playing fair.
   d. Going to a decent college.
   e. Divine right.
5. I always wanted my mother to be . . .
   a. More liberal.
   b. Less nosy.
   c. A better cook.
   d. Young at heart.
   e. Empress dowager.
6. I think people should stand on . . .
   a. Principle.
   b. Firm ground.
   c. Their own two feet.
   d. Tiptoe.
   e. Ceremony.
7. I feel that it is most important to establish . . .
   a. Rapport.
   b. A decent working relationship.
   c. A precedent.
   d. A dynasty.
8. The best things in life are . . .
   a. Free.
   b. Slaves.
9. I would most like to spend Christmas in . . .
   a. Connecticut.
   b. Palm Beach.
   c. Great Gorge.
   d. The Winter Palace.
10. I think men are at their most attractive when . . .
    a. Playing tennis.
    b. Sleeping.
    c. Dancing.
    d. Laughing.
    e. Kneeling.
11. If I could afford an addition to my house I would build . . .
    a. A workshop.
    b. A den.

    c.   A patio.
    d.   A sauna.
    e.   A throne room.

12. I would most like my son to be . . .
    a.   Neat.
    b.   A chip off the old block.
    c.   A doctor.
    d.   Good at sports.
    e.   Crown prince.

13. On a date I most enjoy . . .
    a.   An art film.
    b.   Bowling.
    c.   Dinner and the theater.
    d.   Ruling.

Modern Sports

When it comes to sports I am not particularly interested. Generally speaking, I look upon them as dangerous and tiring activities performed by people with whom I share nothing except the right to trial by jury. It is not that I am totally indifferent to the joys of athletic effort—it is simply that my idea of what constitutes sport does not coincide with popularly held notions on the subject. There are a number of reasons for this, chief among them being that to me the outdoors is what you must pass through in order to get from your apartment into a taxicab.

There *are,* however, several contests in which I *do* engage and not, I might add, without a certain degree of competence. The following is by no means a complete list:

1. Ordering in Some Breakfast.
2. Picking Up the Mail.
3. Going Out for Cigarettes.
4. Meeting for a Drink.

As you can see, these are largely urban activities and, as such, not ordinarily regarded with much respect by sports enthusiasts. Nevertheless, they all require skill, stamina, and courage. And they all have their penalties and their rewards.

There are many such activities and I, for one, feel that the time is ripe for them to receive proper recognition. I therefore propose that those in charge of the 1980 Olympic Games invite New York to participate as a separate entity. The New York team would be entered in only one contest, to be called the New York Decathlon. The New York Decathlon would consist of four events instead of the usual ten, since everyone in New York is very busy. It would further differ from the conventional decathlon in that each contestant would enter only one event, since in New York it pays to specialize. The four events would be Press Agentry, Dry Cleaning and Laundering, Party-going, and Dog-owning.

Traditionally the Olympic Games open with a torch-bearer followed by all the athletes marching around the stadium carrying flags. This will not be changed, but in 1980 the athletes will be followed by seventeen Checker cabs carrying the New York team. The first cabby in line will have his arm out the window and in his hand will be a torch. The passengers in this cab will be screaming at the cabby as sparks fly into the back seat. He will pretend not to hear them. When the parade concludes, the first cabby will fail to notice this immediately and he will be compelled to stop short. This will cause all the following cabs to run into each other. The cabbies will then spend the rest of the Olympics yelling at each other and writing things down in a threatening manner. The athletics teams will be forced to start the games even though this collision has occurred where it will cause the greatest inconvenience.

Press Agentry

The two contestants enter the stadium from opposite sides, having first been assured by the referee that both sides are equally important. They kiss each other on both cheeks and turn smartly toward the crowd. They do not look past the first ten rows. They then seat themselves on facing Ultrasuede sofas and light cigarettes. Two moonlighting ball boys race in with coffee black, no sugar. The contestants pick up their ringing phones. Points awarded as follows:

1. For not taking the most calls from people who wish to speak to you.
2. For waking up the most people who do not.
3. For telling the most people who want to attend an event that they can't have tickets.
4. For telling the most people who do not want to attend said event that you have already sent them tickets by messenger and that they owe you a favor.

Dry Cleaning and Laundering

Two fully equipped dry cleaning and laundering establishments are constructed in inconvenient areas of the stadium. Several innocent people enter each establishment. These people serve the same function in this event that the fox serves in a hunt. They place upon the counters piles of soiled clothing, receive little slips of colored paper, and leave. Points awarded as follows:

1. For ripping off the most buttons.
   a. Additional points if buttons are impossible to replace.
2. For washing the most silk shirts bearing labels stating DRY CLEAN ONLY.
   a. Additional points if shirts are washed with bleeding madras jackets.
   b. If shirts are white, victory is near.

3. For boxing the most shirts requested on hangers.
4. For losing the most garments.
   a. Additional points according to expensiveness of garments.
5. For being the most ingenious in moving ink spots from one pant leg to the other.

Party-going

A room exactly half the size necessary is built in the center of the stadium. Too many contestants enter the room. Points awarded as follows:

1. For getting to the bar.
2. For getting away from the bar.
3. For accidentally spilling wine on an opponent to whom you have lost a job.
4. For inadvertently dropping a hot cigarette ash on same.
5. For making the greatest number of funny remarks about people not present.
6. For arriving the latest with the greatest number of famous people.
7. For leaving the earliest with an old lover's new flame.

Dog-owning

There has been erected in the stadium an exact replica of a fifteen-block section of Greenwich Village. Twenty contestants leave buildings on the perimeter of this area, each walking three dogs who have not been out of the house all day. The object of the game is to be the first to get to the sidewalk directly in front of my building.

When all of the points are added up, the contestant with the greatest number of points enters the stadium. He is followed by the two contestants with the next greatest number of points. The two runners-up go off to one side with the referee. The referee takes out a stop-watch. Each runner-up has five minutes in which to explain in an entertaining manner why *he* did not receive the most points. Whichever runner-up is the more arrogant and convincing is presented with the gold medal. Because in New York it's not whether you win or lose—it's how you lay the blame.

Breeding Will Tell:
A Family Treatment

There once appeared in a magazine a photograph of myself taken under obviously youthful circumstances. I assumed that it would be readily apparent to all that this was my high school yearbook picture. I neglected, however, to take into consideration that I number among my acquaintances some people of decidedly lofty background. I was first jarred into awareness of this by a well-born young fashion model who, in reference to said photograph, offered, "I really loved your deb picture, Fran." Had that been the end of it I would undoubtedly have forgotten the incident, but later on that very same evening an almost identical remark was made by a minor member of the Boston aristocracy. As far as I was concerned this constituted a trend. I therefore felt faced with a decision: either snort derisively at the very idea or create an amusing fiction appropriate to such thinking. Being at least peripherally in the amusing fiction business, I chose the latter and thus have prepared the following genealogy.

Margaret Lebovitz, my paternal grandmother, was born in Ghetto Point, Hungary (a restricted community), at the very dawn of the Gay Nineties. An appealing child, she was often left in the care of trusted family retainers (my Aunt Sadie and Uncle Benny), as her father's far-flung business affairs—which were mainly concerned with being conscripted into the army—frequently kept him away from home. Although her mother spent most of her time amusing herself in the cabbage fields, she nevertheless made it a point to visit the nursery every evening and stand guard while little Margaret said her prayers. Margaret's childhood was a happy one—she and her chums exchanged confidences and babushkas as they whiled away the carefree hours picking beets and playing hide and seek with the Cossacks. Tariff, the family estate, where the Lebovitzes wintered (*and* summered) was indeed a wondrous place and it was therefore not surprising when Margaret balked at being sent away to school. Her father, home on a brief desertion, took her into his straw-lined study—which was affectionately called "Daddy's hideout"—and explained patiently that unbreakable tradition demanded that girls of Margaret's class acquire the necessary social graces such as fleeing demurely and staying properly alive. Margaret listened respectfully and agreed to begin her freshman year at Miss Belief's.

Margaret was a great success at Miss Belief's, where her taste in footwear quickly won her the nickname Bootsie. Bootsie was an excellent student and demonstrated such a flair for barely audible breathing that she was unanimously elected chairman of the Spring Day Escape Committee. That is not to say that Bootsie was a grind—quite the contrary. An irrepressible madcap, Bootsie got herself into such bad scrapes that the fellow members of her club, the Huddled Masses, were frequently compelled to come to her rescue. Fond of outdoor sports, Bootsie longed for summer vacation and happily joined in the girlish cries of "Serf's up!" that greeted the season.

Upon reaching her eighteenth birthday, Bootsie made her debut into society and her beauty, charm, and way with a hoe soon gained her a reputation as the Brenda Frazier of Ghetto Point. All of the young men in her set were smitten with Bootsie and found it absolutely necessary to secure the promise of a waltz days in advance of a party, as her dance pogrom was invariably full. Bootsie's favorite beau was Tibor, a tall, dashing young deserter and two-time winner of the Hungarian Cup Race, which was held yearly in a lavishly irrigated wheat field. Tibor was fond of Bootsie, but he was not unmindful of the fact that she would one day come into her father's great plowshare, and this was his primary interest in her. The discovery that Tibor was a fortune hunter had a devastating effect upon Bootsie and she took to her bed. Bootsie's family, understandably concerned about her condition, held a meeting to discuss the problem. It was concluded that a change of scenery would do her a world of good. A plan of action was decided upon and thus Bootsie Lebovitz was sent steerage to Ellis Island in order that she might forget.

Disco Hints:
The New Etiquette

It may come as somewhat of a surprise to those who know me only as a woman of letters to learn that I am quite fond of dancing and not half bad at it either. I am not, however, fond of large groups of people. This is unfortunate, for it is not feasible to bring into one's own home all of the desirable accoutrements of discothèque dancing such as a deejay, several hours of tape, and the possibility, slim as it might be, of meeting one's own true love. I am therefore compelled to spend night after night amongst hordes of strangers, many of whom conduct themselves without the slightest regard for the sensibilities of their fellow dancers. This has led me to compile a short list of helpful tips to ensure more pleasant dancing for all.

1. When the discothèque in question is a private club with a strict members-only policy, it is not good form to stand outside and beg in an unattractive tone of voice to be taken in. It is even less appealing to threaten the life or reputation of an entering member with either a knife or the information that you know his real

name and are planning on phoning his hometown newspaper with the true reason why he hasn't married.

2. There is no question but that after a few moments of dancing you are likely to become quite warm. This should not be taken as a cue to remove your shirt. If one of your fellow dancers should be interested in your progress at the gym, rest assured that he will not be too shy to ask. Should you find the heat unbearable you can just take that bandanna out of your back pocket and blot your forehead. Just be sure you put it back on the right side.

3. If you are of the opinion that an evening without amyl nitrate is like a day without sunshine, you should avail yourself of this substance in the privacy of your own truck and not in the middle of a crowded dance floor.

4. If you are a disc jockey, kindly remember that your job is to play records that people will enjoy dancing to and not to impress possible visiting disc jockeys with your esoteric taste. People generally enjoy dancing to songs that have words and are of a reasonable length. Sixteen-minute instrumentals by West African tribal drummers are frequently the cause of undue amyl nitrate consumption and shirt removal.

Better Read Than Dead:
A Revised Opinion

My attendance at grammar school coincided rather unappealingly with the height of the cold war. This resulted in my spending a portion of each day sitting cross-legged, head in lap, either alone under my desk or, more sociably, against the wall in the corridor. When not so occupied I could be found sitting in class reading avidly about the horrors of life under Communism. I was not a slow child, but I believed passionately that Communists were a race of horned men who divided their time equally between the burning of Nancy Drew books and the devising of a plan of nuclear attack that would land the largest and most lethal bomb squarely upon the third-grade class of Thomas Jefferson School in Morristown, New Jersey. This was a belief widely held among my classmates and it was reinforced daily by teachers and those parents who were of the Republican persuasion.

Among the many devices used to keep this belief alive was a detailed chart that appeared yearly in our social studies book. This chart pointed out the severe economic hardships of Communist life. The reading aloud of the chart was accompanied by a running commentary from the teacher and went something like this:

"This chart shows how long a man must work in Russia in order to purchase the following goods. We then compare this to the length of time it takes a man in the United States to earn enough money to purchase the same goods."

RUSSIA	U.S.A.

A PAIR OF SHOES—38 HOURS

"And they only have brown oxfords in Russia, so that nobody ever gets to wear shoes without straps even for dress-up. Also they have never even heard of Capezios, and if they did, no one would be allowed to wear them because they all have to work on farms whenever they are not busy making atom bombs."

A PAIR OF SHOES—2 HOURS

"And we have all kinds of shoes, even Pappagallos."

A LOAF OF BREAD—2½ HOURS

"They do not have peanut butter in Russia, or Marshmallow Fluff, and their bread has a lot of crust on it, which they force all the children to eat."

A LOAF OF BREAD—5 MINUTES

"We have cinnamon raisin bread and english muffins and we can put whatever we like on it because we have democracy."

A POUND OF NAILS—6 HOURS

"And they need a lot of nails in Russia because everyone has to work very hard all the time building things—even mothers."

A POUND OF NAILS—8 MINUTES

"Even though we don't need that many nails because we have Scotch tape and staples."

A STATION WAGON—9 YEARS

"If they were even permitted to own them, which they are not, so everyone has to walk everywhere even though they are very tired from building so many things like atom bombs."

A STATION WAGON—4 MONTHS

"And we have so many varieties to choose from—some painted to look like wood on the sides and some that are two different colors. We also have lots of other cars, such as convertible sports cars."

A PAIR OF OVERALLS—11 HOURS

"And everyone has to wear overalls all the time and they're all the same color so nobody gets to wear straight skirts even if they're in high school."

A PAIR OF OVERALLS—1 HOUR

"But since we can choose what we want to wear in a democracy, mostly farmers wear overalls and they like to wear them."

A DOZEN EGGS—7 HOURS

"But they hardly ever get to eat them because eggs are a luxury in Russia and there are no luxuries under Communism."

A DOZEN EGGS—9 MINUTES

"We have lots of eggs here and that is why we can have eggnog, egg salad, even Easter eggs, except for the Jewish children in the class, who I'm sure have something just as nice on their holiday, which is called Hanukkah."

A TELEVISION SET—2 YEARS

"But they don't have them. That's right, they do not have TV in Russia because they know that if the people in Russia were allowed to watch *Leave It to Beaver* they would all want to move to the United States, and probably most of them would want to come to Morristown."

A TELEVISION SET—2 WEEKS

"And many people have two television sets and some people like Dougie Bershey have color TV so that he can tell everyone in class what color everything was on *Walt Disney.*"

All of this was duly noted by both myself and my classmates, and the vast majority of us were rather right-wing all through grammar school. Upon reaching adolescence, however, a number of us rebelled and I must admit to distinctly leftist leanings during my teen years. Little by little, though, I have been coming around to my former way of thinking and, while I am not all that enamored of our local form of government, I have reacquired a marked distaste for Theirs.

My political position is based largely on my aversion to large groups, and if there's one thing I know about Communism it's that large groups are definitely in the picture. I do not work well with others and I do not wish to learn to do so. I do not even dance well with others if there are too many of them, and I have no doubt but that Communist discothèques are hideously overcrowded. "From each according to his ability, to each according to his needs" is not a decision I care to leave to politicians, for I do not believe that an ability to remark humorously on the passing scene would carry much weight with one's comrades or that one could convince them of the need for a really reliable answering service. The common good is not my cup of tea—it is the uncommon good in which I am interested, and I do not deceive myself that such statements are much admired by the members of farming collectives. Communists all seem to wear small caps, a look I consider better suited to tubes of toothpaste than to people. We number, of course, among us our own cap wearers, but I assure you they are easily avoided. It is my understanding that Communism requires of its adherents that they arise early and participate in a strenuous round of calisthenics. To someone who wishes that cigarettes came already lit the thought of such exertion at any hour when decent people are just nodding off is thoroughly abhorrent. I have been further advised that in the Communist world an aptitude for speaking or writing in an amusing fashion doesn't count for spit. I therefore have every intention of doing my best to keep the Iron Curtain from

being drawn across Fifty-seventh Street. It is to this end
that I have prepared a little chart of my own for the
edification of my fellow New Yorkers.

The following chart compares the amount of time it
takes a Communist to earn enough to purchase the following goods against the amount of time it takes a New
Yorker to do the same.

COMMUNIST	NEW YORKER
A CO-OP APARTMENT IN THE EAST SEVENTIES ON THE PARK—4,000 YEARS. And even then you have to share it with the rest of the collective. There is not a co-op in the city with that many bathrooms.	A CO-OP APARTMENT IN THE EAST SEVENTIES ON THE PARK—No time at all if you were lucky in the parent department. If you have not been so blessed it could take as long as twenty years, but at least you'd have your own bathroom.
A SUBSCRIPTION TO *The New Yorker*—3 WEEKS. And even then it is doubtful that you'd understand the cartoons.	A SUBSCRIPTION TO *The New Yorker*—1 HOUR, maybe less, because in a democracy one frequently receives such things as gifts.
A FIRST-CLASS AIRPLANE TICKET TO PARIS—6 MONTHS—Paris, Comrade? Not so fast.	A FIRST-CLASS AIRPLANE TICKET TO PARIS—Varies widely, but any smart girl can acquire such a ticket with ease if she plays her cards right.
A FERNANDO SANCHEZ NIGHT-GOWN—3 MONTHS. With the cap? Very attractive.	A FERNANDO SANCHEZ NIGHT-GOWN—1 WEEK, less if you know someone in the busi-ness, and need I point out that your chances of being so con-nected are far greater in a de-mocracy such as ours than they are in Peking.

DINNER AT A FINE RESTAURANT—
2 YEARS to earn the money; 27 years for the collective to decide on a restaurant.

DINNER AT A FINE RESTAURANT—
No problem if one has chosen one's friends wisely.

Children:
Pro or Con?

Moving, as I do, in what would kindly be called artistic circles, children are an infrequent occurrence. But even the most artistic of circles includes within its periphery a limited edition of the tenaciously domestic.

As I am generally quite fond of children I accept this condition with far less displeasure than do my more rarefied acquaintances. That is not to imply that I am a total fool for a little grin but simply that I consider myself to be in a position of unquestionable objectivity and therefore eminently qualified to deal with the subject in an authoritative manner.

From the number of children in evidence it appears that people have them at the drop of a hat—for surely were they to give this matter its due attention they would act with greater decorum. Of course, until now prospective parents have not had the opportunity to see the facts spelled out in black and white and therefore cannot reasonably be held accountable for their actions. To this end I have carefully set down all pertinent information in the fervent hope that it will result in a future populated by a more attractive array of children than I have thus far encountered.

Pro

I must take issue with the term "a mere child," for it has been my invariable experience that the company of a mere child is infinitely preferable to that of a mere adult.

* * *

Children are usually small in stature, which makes them quite useful for getting at those hard-to-reach places.

* * *

Children do not sit next to one in restaurants and discuss their preposterous hopes for the future in loud tones of voice.

* * *

Children ask better questions than do adults. "May I have a cookie?" "Why is the sky blue?" and "What does a cow say?" are far more likely to elicit a cheerful response than "Where's your manuscript?" "Why haven't you called?" and "Who's your lawyer?"

* * *

Children give life to the concept of immaturity.

* * *

Children make the most desirable opponents in Scrabble as they are both easy to beat and fun to cheat.

* * *

It is still quite possible to stand in a throng of children without once detecting even the faintest whiff of an exciting, rugged after-shave or cologne.

* * *

Not a single member of the under-age set has yet to propose the word *chairchild.*

* * *

Children sleep either alone or with small toy animals. The wisdom of such behavior is unquestionable, as it frees them from the immeasurable tedium of being privy to the whispered confessions of others. I have yet to run across a teddy bear who was harboring the secret desire to wear a maid's uniform.

Con

Even when freshly washed and relieved of all obvious confections, children tend to be sticky. One can only assume that this has something to do with not smoking enough.

* * *

Children have decidedly little fashion sense and if left to their own devices will more often than not be drawn to garments of unfortunate cut. In this respect they do not differ greatly from the majority of their elders, but somehow one blames them more.

* * *

Children respond inadequately to sardonic humor and veiled threats.

* * *

Notoriously insensitive to subtle shifts in mood, children will persist in discussing the color of a recently sighted cement-mixer long after one's own interest in the topic has waned.

* * *

Children are rarely in the position to lend one a truly interesting sum of money. There are, however, exceptions, and such children are an excellent addition to any party.

* * *

Children arise at an unseemly hour and are ofttimes in the habit of putting food on an empty stomach.

* * *

Children do not look well in evening clothes.

* * *

All too often children are accompanied by adults.

A Manual:
Training for Landlords

Every profession requires of its members certain skills, talents, or training. Dancers must be light on their feet. Brain surgeons must attend medical school. Candlestick-makers must have an affinity for wax. These occupations, though, are only the tip of the iceberg. How do others learn their trades? We shall see.

How to Be a Landlord: An Introduction

In order to be a landlord, it is first necessary to acquire a building or buildings. This can be accomplished in either of two ways. By far the most pleasant is by means of inheritance—a method favored not only because it is easy on the pocketbook but also because it eliminates the tedious chore of selecting the property. This manual, however, is not really intended for landlords of that stripe, since such an inheritance invariably includes a genetic composition that makes formal instruction quite superfluous.

Less attractive but somewhat more common (how

often those traits go hand in hand) is the method of actual purchase. And it is here that our work really begins.

Lesson One: Buying

Buildings can be divided into two main groups: cheap and expensive. It should be remembered, however, that these terms are for professional use only and never to be employed in the presence of tenants, who, almost without exception, prefer the words *very* and *reasonable.* If the price of a building strikes you as excessive, you would do well to consider that wise old slogan "It's not the initial cost—it's the upkeep," for as landlord you are in the enviable position of having entered a profession in which the upkeep is taken care of by the customer. This concept may be somewhat easier to grasp by simply thinking of yourself as a kind of telephone company. You will be further encouraged when you realize that while there may indeed be a wide disparity in building prices, this terrible inequity need not be passed on to the tenant in the degrading form of lower rent. It should now be clear to the attentive student that choosing a building is basically a matter of personal taste and, since it is the rare landlord who is troubled by such a quality, we shall proceed to the next lesson.

Lesson Two: Rooms

The most important factor here is that you understand that a room is a matter of opinion. It is, after all, your building, and if you choose to designate a given amount of space as a room, then indeed it *is* a room. Specifying the function of the room is also your responsibility, and tenants need frequently to be reminded of this as they will all too often display a tendency to call one of your rooms a closet. This is, of course, a laughable pretension, since few tenants have ever seen a closet.

Lesson Three: Walls

A certain number of walls are one of the necessary evils of the business. And while some of you will understandably bridle at the expense, the observant student is aware that walls offer a good return on investment by way of providing one of the basic components of rooms. That is not to say that you, as landlord, must be a slave to convention. Plaster and similarly substantial materials are embarrassingly passé to the progressive student. If you are a father, you know that walls can enjoyably be made by children at home or camp with a simple paste of flour and water and some of Daddy's old newspapers. The childless landlord might well be interested in Wallies—a valuable new product that comes on a roll. Wallies tear off easily and *can* be painted, should such a procedure ever be enforced by law.

Lesson Four: Heat

The arrival of winter seems invariably to infect the tenant with an almost fanatical lust for warmth. Sweaters and socks he may have galore; yet he refuses to perceive their usefulness and stubbornly and selfishly insists upon obtaining *his* warmth through *your* heat. There are any number of ploys available to the resourceful landlord, but the most effective requires an actual cash outlay. No mind, it's well worth it—fun, too. Purchase a tape recorder. Bring the tape recorder to your suburban home and place it in the vicinity of your heater. Here its sensitive mechanism will pick up the sounds of impending warmth. This recording played at high volume in

the basement of the building has been known to sty-
mie tenants for days on end.

Lesson Five: Water

It is, of course, difficult for the landlord to understand
the tenant's craving for water when the modern super-
market is fairly bursting with juices and soft drinks of
every description. The burden is made no easier by the
fact that at least some of the time this water must be hot.
The difficult situation is only partially alleviated by the
knowledge that *hot,* like *room,* is a matter of opinion.

Lesson Six: Roaches

It is the solemn duty of every landlord to maintain an
adequate supply of roaches. The minimum acceptable
roach to tenant ratio is four thousand to one. Should this
arrangement prompt an expression of displeasure on
the part of the tenant, ignore him absolutely. The tenant
is a notorious complainer. Just why this is so is not certain, though a number of theories abound. The most
plausible of these ascribes the tenant's chronic irritabil-
ity to his widely suspected habit of drinking enormous
quantities of heat and hot water—a practice well known
to result in the tragically premature demise of hallway
light bulbs.

Success Without College

The term *stage mother* is used to describe a female parent who, to put it kindly, has taken it upon herself to instill in her child theatrical ambition and eventual success. The entire upbringing of the child has this goal as its basis and has undoubtedly resulted in the creation of more than a few stars.

Ours, however, is an age of specialization and keen competition and it is naive to assume that this sort of childrearing technique is confined to the world of show business. Below are some examples:

The Architecture Mother

The architecture mother does indeed have her work cut out for her. Her days are filled with the difficult task of impressing upon her youngster the need for economy of line and the desirability of wiping one's feet before coming into the machine for living. Other mothers have children who pay attention, who realize that form should follow function, and that there's such a thing as considering the reflective qualities of glass *before* going out to play. Other mothers can relax once in a while because their children listen the *first* time without having to be told over and over again, until I'm sick of hearing myself say it, *"Less, less, I mean it, less.* And I'm *not* going to say it again."

The Television Talk Show Host Mother

Here is a job that presents such a multiplicity of problems that relatively few have entered the field. The work is arduous and the hours long, for it is still too soon to tell whether the child will be early morning, mid-afternoon, or late night. Hardly a facet of modern life can be disregarded. "Vegas, darling, the 'Las' is strictly for *them.* Just plain Vegas. That's right. Now what do we do in Vegas? No, darling, that's what *they* do in Vegas. *We play* Vegas. We *are playing* Vegas. We *played* Vegas. Let's not forget our grammar. Let's have a little consideration for the English language here, please. Now, when we play Vegas what else do we do? That's right—*kill them. Kill them* in Vegas. *Killing them* in Vegas. *Killed them* in Vegas. And what do we do when things get interesting? Well, yes, we can bleep sometimes, but that's not what pays allowances, is it? That's not what buys bicycles. No. We sell a little something. We cut to a commercial. We have a word from our sponsors and we break the stations. Good. Now, here's a book. What do we do with books? No, and I don't want to have to say it again, *we* don't read books. You want to read books or you want to be a television talk show host? You can't have it both ways. We don't *read* books. We *mean* to read books. And where do we mean to read books? That's right—*on the plane. We meant to read it on the plane.* And why didn't we? Come on, we've been through this a thousand times. I'll give you a hint—but this is the last time. O.K., here's the hint—it starts with *D.* That's right, Duke. We meant to read it on the plane but we ran into the Duke—Duke Wayne. Very good, darling, terriffic. I think that's enough for tonight. Just a minute, young man, where do you think *you're* going? To bed? Really? Without a quick rundown of tomorrow night's guests? That's how you leave a room? Very nice. Excellent. Eighteen hours a day with this and you just leave the room without a quick rundown of tomorrow night's guests. That's no way to be a television talk show host and if you don't learn now you're going to find out later the hard way. *I mean it.* I don't like to say it—I *am* your mother—but you're going to be canceled, I mean it. What? Who? Cloris Leachman? Gore Vidal? Shecky Green? Dr. Joyce Brothers and Jim Bouton? That's my baby. You're a beautiful guy, darling. Good night."

The Mortician Mother

The burden borne by the mortician mother is not an easy one. For she must spend virtually every waking hour policing the behavior of her child. Is that *giggling* she hears? Wearily she must go to his room and admonish him for the ten thousandth time, "Could you look a little somber, please? I mean, is that too much to ask? A little dignity? A little sorrowful understanding? Other kids manage to look somber without having to be told every twenty seconds. Other kids can be trusted alone for ten minutes without a lot of laughter. Other kids don't shrug their shoulders and walk away when their mothers ask for a little opinion on how they look—other kids say, 'Very lifelike' in a nice hushed tone the first time they're asked. Other kids can wear a carnation a whole day without it wilting. I don't know where I went wrong with you. I don't know where you got this taste for simplicity, not even simplicity: just ordinary cheapness if you ask me. Oh yes, don't think I don't know about that plain pine box you've got in here. I'm not stupid. Well, let me tell you something, Mr. Know-It-All. There is such a thing as solid mahogany with real brass fittings and satin lining and the sooner you learn that the better off you'll be."

The Headwaiter Mother

Few appreciate the problems that beset the mother of the aspiring headwaiter. Not only has she to contend with the difficulty of instilling in him a passion for the unnecessary flourish but she must also curb his every naïve instinct for friendliness. "How many times have I told you not to answer the first time you're spoken to? *How many?* And what is this *helpful business* all of a sudden, may I ask? Where did you pick *that* up? Is *that* what you want to be when you grow up? *Helpful?* Fine. Wonderful. Go, be helpful. Be a Boy Scout for all I care. Yes, a Boy Scout—because that's how you'll end up if you don't stop fooling around. *I'm* not the one who wants to be a headwaiter. I'm not the one who said, 'Oh, Mommy, if you mold me into a headwaiter I'll never ask you for another thing, not ever.' So I'm not the one who'll suffer. You want to be a headwaiter? *Act* like a headwaiter. A little ignoring, please. A little uncalled-for arrogance. You want to be obsequious? Believe me, there's a time and a place. Princess Grace comes in, David Rockefeller, Tennessee Williams, O.K., fine, good, *then* be obsequious—you have my blessing. But I don't want to see it all the time. I don't want to see it for some expense account jerk who's out on the town. I don't want to see it for every leisure suit with two on the aisle for *A Chorus Line.* Understand? A little more influence peddling and a little less with the warm welcome, O.K.? Your father and I aren't going to be here forever, you know."

The Restaurant Critic Mother

The restaurant critic mother is a proud woman. So proud, in fact, that those who know her have pretty much had it up to here with listening to what a picky eater she's got on her hands. But her pride is understandable, for she has earned it. For years she has asked, "How was lunch, dear?" only to be answered with a terse "O.K." Over and over again she has drilled her little charge until the happy day when her question elicits this rewarding response: "Mommy, the sandwich was superb. The Wonder Bread softly unobtrusive, the perfect foil for both the richly poignant Superchunky Skippy and the clear, fragrant Welch's grape. The carrot sticks were exquisitely sweet, yet asserted their integrity in every glorious crunch. The Yoo Hoo was interesting—adolescent but robust—and the Yankee Doodle, a symphony of snowy creme filling and rich, dark cake; the whole of it bathed in a splendor of chocolate-flavored icing that verged on the sinful."

Specialty Banking:
A Numbered Account

Not so long ago, in Manhattan's fashionable East Fifties, there appeared an institution called the First Women's Bank. This prompted me to speculate:

1. Is this a mere fad or an actual trend?
2. What is the First Women's Bank really like?
3. Can we look forward to the opening of a competitive establishment to be known as the Other Women's Bank?

I have mulled this over and have been successful in formulating answers to all three questions. My original intention was to answer these questions in order, but I eventually chose another plan of action. Lest you get the wrong impression, I hasten to assure you that this in no way constitutes a flamboyant display of perversity. It is simply that I changed my mind—which is, after all, a woman's prerogative.

What Is the First Women's Bank Really Like?

Rather than attempt to answer this question by utilizing the methods of the investigative reporter—legwork, research, and digging for facts—I decided instead to employ those of the irresponsible wag: lying on the sofa, talking on the phone, and making things up. This procedure proved quite satisfactory and has resulted in the following report.

The First Women's Bank is called the First Women's Bank only in deference to convention. It is not the real name. The real name is Separate Checks. When a typical customer (for the purposes of clarity we'll call her Jane Doe) enters the bank she has three windows from which to choose:

1. PAYING: BACK
2. IS: RECEIVING
3. NO: ACCOUNTING: FOR TASTE

Should Jane find these departments inadequate for her needs and experience a momentary loss of faith, she has only to remember that her bank offers every possible convenience—a Christmas Club, a Hanukkah Club, and a Bridge Club—in order to regain her former confidence. Thus fortified, even the knowledge that the bank closes two or three days a month for cramps will not deter her from venturing into the area reserved for a more serious business. Here she will be confronted by a neat row of desks, each sporting a dignified oblong nameplate: Madge, Delores, Wilma, and Mary Beth respectively. Jane chooses Mary Beth and sits down. Mary Beth pours Jane a cup of coffee, apologizes for the state of her blotter, and asks Jane what's bothering her. When Jane asks Mary Beth how she knew something was bothering her, Mary Beth just smiles and says, "Woman's intuition." Jane explains to Mary Beth that she needs to borrow eleven hundred dollars to repair her car, which was severely damaged in an accident resulting from Jane's attempt to execute a sharp right turn while applying lip gloss. Jane is eager to have the car fixed before her husband returns from his business trip. Mary Beth understands, of course, and an arrangement is made whereby Separate Checks agrees to lend Jane eleven hundred dollars if Jane will lend Separate Checks eight place settings of her good silver for their next board luncheon. Her business successfully concluded, Jane takes her leave—happily reciting the bank's catchy slogan, "Bottom Dollar: Tops to Match." She is eleven hundred dollars richer and more firmly convinced than ever that Separate Checks is the permanent wave of the future.

Is This a Mere Fad or an Actual Trend?

The answer to this question is "An actual trend." The success of Separate Checks will cause an outbreak of specialty banks, each catering to an extremely specific group.

Children

This institution will be called the First National Piggy Bank. It will offer to its customers a unique service— Banking by Color. It will be fully equipped with high-quality crayons, which will be attached to anchored chains. The bank's motto will be "Our Checks Bounce Higher Than Yours Do," and instead of patterns, its checks will be available in a variety of flavors: Red Raspberry, Chocolate Marshmallow, Vanilla Fudge, and Black Cherry. The employees will be kind but firm, and those dealing with the more intricate procedures such as Advance on Next Week's Allowance Loans will sit behind desks bearing their nameplates—Uncle Ralph, Aunt Marcia, Uncle Harold, and Auntie Ruthie. Should one of the customers default on such a loan he will be sent to his room without dessert for 6½ percent of each month he is overdue. If this fails to bring about the desired result the bank will have no recourse but to garnishee the debtor's birthday money until the loan is repaid. Hours: After School and On the Weekend When the Homework Is Finished.

Homosexuals

The First National Raving Bank will distinguish itself by being the only bank in town with a two-drink minimum. Special features include the availability of three-dollar bills and checks bearing either a portrait of Ronald Firbank or all of the lyrics to "Somewhere over the Rainbow." Should a customer of the bank wish to apply for a credit card he need only enter the business area, where he will find Mr. Eugene, Mr. Randy, Mr. Joel, and Eduardo, ready and willing to furnish him with the information that Master Charge isn't the only game in town. Hours: After.

Psychiatrists

The New York Bank of Self-Pity will not be housed in a single building but rather in a complex, since nothing is that simple. If one of the customers is overdrawn he can attempt to convince the bank to make good his check, as it was their inability to deal realistically with figures that caused the error. If he is desirous of establishing a more meaningful relationship with his account he is free to lie down and discuss it with one of the self-destructive and immature employees. The pens in this bank are thoughtfully equipped with ink that blots symbolically. Hours: 10:10–10:50.

Can We Look Forward to the Opening of a Competitive Establishment to Be Known as the Other Women's Bank?

Undoubtedly. The telltale signs will be safety deposit boxes filled with expensive baubles, a sultry look, and a tendency to be alone at Christmas. Hours: Tuesday and Thursday Afternoons.

The Right of Eminent Domain Versus the Rightful Dominion of the Eminent

Generally speaking, laws are designed to protect the public from harm. Generally speaking, harm is seen as physical peril: Generally speaking, physical peril is not a particularly interesting subject. True, there are those laws which endeavor to shield the public from financial disaster. Truer still, financial disaster occurs anyway. And truest of all, the public is not a particularly interesting group.

Thus our system of law is something less than captivating, for it consistently fails to deal with the three questions of greatest concern. The three questions of greatest concern are:

1. Is it attractive?
2. Is it amusing?
3. Does it know its place?

One can see at a glance that these three questions not only encompass all contingencies covered by the present system but, more importantly, they confront without flinching the genuine hazards of modern life. They are therefore the only possible basis for any reasonable system of justice. And henceforth they shall be regarded as such. If you must reply in the negative to any of these questions you are committing an illegal act. For the purposes of clarity I shall consider each question separately, although it should be quite apparent that they are all three as brothers.

Is It Attractive?

When I was in grammar school it was customary at the beginning of each year for the teacher to explain the principle of individual freedom in a democracy by stating: "Your right to swing your arm ends where the other person's nose begins." An admirable sentiment— unquestionably. But one somehow lacking in that little something extra that makes it all worthwhile.

Quite simply, it misses the point. I, for one, would much rather be punched in the nose than in the sensibility. And so I offer this in its stead: "Your right to wear a mint-green polyester leisure suit ends where it meets my eye." Should you choose to disregard this dictate you shall be arrested for bad taste.

In order to administer to all of the worms that will come crawling out of this hitherto unopened can there will be appointed a Commissar of Good Looks who shall issue a manifesto detailing the following offenses:

    A. The Construction of Buildings That Look Like Gigantic Electric Shavers.

    B. Television Commercials and Magazine Advertisements That Use Real People Instead of Models.

    C. Cigarettes That Come in a Choice of Colors: If White Ones Were Good Enough for Edward R. Murrow They're Good Enough for You.

    D. Ice Cubes That Come in a Choice of Shapes: Flowers Belong in One's Lapel, Not in One's Bourbon.

    E. Airports That Have Fallen into the Hands of Graphic Designers with a Penchant for Bold Simplicity.

F. Furniture Made to Resemble Objects That Were Played with by Small Children in the Nineteen-Forties.

G. Long-sleeved T-Shirts Stenciled to Look Like Dinner Jackets and Invariably Worn by Those Who Would Have Occasion to Wear a Dinner Jacket Only While at Work.

The penalty for those responsible for any of the above-mentioned crimes shall be ninety days spent in the company of the inventor of the male centerfold or seventy-two months in Los Angeles—whichever comes first.

Is It Amusing?

Once upon a time, long, long ago, people wanted to be well spoken. Those capable of an elegant turn of phrase were much admired. Wit was in great demand. It was the day of the epigram.

Time went on, and by and by it came to pass that people were chiefly interested in being well liked. Those capable of a firm handshake were much admired. Friendliness was in great demand. It was the day of the telegram.

Presently it appears that people are mainly concerned with being well rested. Those capable of uninterrupted sleep are much admired. Unconsciousness is in great demand. This is the day of the milligram.

Far be it from me to make noise while you're asleep but I should like to notify you that you are under arrest for being boring. The Commissar of a Way with Words suspects you of one or more of the following:

A. Rather Than Attempt the Art of Conversation You Prefer to Communicate with Your Fellow Man by Hugging Strangers Who Are Reliving the Bad Parts of Their Childhood While Immersed in a Swimming Pool Filled with Warm Water.

B. You Think That the Women's Liberation Movement *Does* Have a Sense of Humor.

C. You Use in Conversation Phrases That Appear on
   T-Shirts.
D. You Share David Susskind's Apparently Inexhausti-
   ble Interest in the Private Lives of Deservedly Un-
   known Homosexuals.
E. You Feel the Need to Discuss Your Innermost
   Thoughts on a Weekly Basis with Six Other People,
   One of Whom Is Being Paid to Listen.
F. You No Longer Feel the Need to Discuss Your Inner-
   most Thoughts on a Weekly Basis with Six Other Peo-
   ple, One of Whom Is Being Paid to Listen, Because
   You Feel That Erica Jong Has Said It All for You.
G. The Letters est Have Meaning for You Beyond East-
   ern Standard Time.
H. You Are the Host of a Television Talk Show Who So
   Firmly Believes That Everyone in the Whole World
   Is Just About to Play Las Vegas for Two Weeks That
   You Introduce Your Next Guest as "Dr. Jonas Salk—
   a Beautiful Guy."

Should you be found guilty you shall be sentenced to
a one-year subscription to *Psychology Today* or seventy-
two months in Los Angeles—whichever comes first.

Does It Know Its Place?

Under the jurisdiction of the Commissar of What Is
Appropriate the adage "A place for everything and everything in its place" has been broadened to include "A
place for everyone and everyone in their place." You are
not in your place or are responsible for something not
being in *its* place if you are to blame in any of these
instances:

A. You Are a Man Who Attends Consciousness-raising
   Meetings.
B. You Are a Woman Who Attends Consciousness-rais-
   ing Meetings.
C. You Are a Dog and You Live in New York, Probably
   in My Neighborhood.

D. You Are an Army Camouflage Combat Uniform Being Worn by Someone Who Is Not a Soldier in Southeast Asia.

E. You Are Wall-to-Wall Carpeting and You Are in the Bathroom.

F. You Are on Your Way over to My Apartment and You Have Not Called First.

G. You Write Poetry and You Are Not Dead.

Those convicted of any of the above-mentioned crimes shall be subject to being either a dessert served in a brandy snifter or seventy-two months in Los Angeles—whichever comes first.

The Family Affair:
A Moral Tale

The addition of the prefix *natural* to the word *childbirth* assumed that there was such a thing as unnatural childbirth. Advocates of this concept pointed out that for thousands of years people had babies in the privacy and quietude of their own homes or rice paddies simply by lying down and breathing deeply. This business of rushing to the hospital, being shot up with drugs, and attended by doctors was wrong. It was not meant to be. Some listened. Some did not. Some of those who did not, did not arrogantly, with a strong, pure belief in the righteousness of their unnaturalness. They liked rushing to the hospital. They loved being shot up with drugs. They adored being attended to by doctors. To them unnaturalness was the way of life. Secure in their commitment to artificiality, they greeted each other with knowing looks and bade each other good-bye with a whispered "à rebours." They were content and they believed themselves to be as sophisticated as was possible under the circumstances, which were undeniably heterosexual and therefore limited.

Then little by little there began to circulate among

this group an unsettling rumor. Dark mutterings were heard. The fast crowd was seen less and less frequently in the better waiting rooms. After months of hushed speculation the truth was uncovered: a certain chichi element had found a way to have children that made mere unnatural childbirth look like eating your own placenta. This set had entirely dispensed with bodily function and were obtaining their children in bars.

The most popular of these bars was called Chicken Little and was located in a brownstone on a fashionable street near the East River. Prospective parents on the prowl would arrive at this establishment by taxi or private car, knock smartly on the lacquered chocolate-brown door, and present themselves to a deceptively kind-looking septuagenarian known only as the Grandmother.

Upon passing muster, they either sat at small tables or leaned against the bar and tried to look loving as they cruised the children. They talked very little and then only to remark on the quality of the trade with such comments as "Think he looks like me?" "There's a student council president if I ever saw one," and "Do you think she'll make her bed?" The most aggressive were known to sidle right up to promising-looking tots and murmur, "Like to play catch, fella?" Or to take particularly blond little girls aside, slip them homemade chocolate chip cookies, and let them know in no uncertain terms that there were plenty more where those came from.

The children were not without ploys of their own and some of the little tykes would stop at nothing. As the evening wore on and most of the really permissive-looking adults had been picked off, it was not uncommon for the desperate unadopted to be seen furtively applying calculatingly cute arrays of freckles across the bridges of their little noses with cleverly concealed brown eyebrow pencils, or announcing in loud, bound-to-be-over-heard voices that when they grew up they wanted to be doctors.

No careful observer of this scene could help but notice that certain patrons bypassed the main area and headed immediately for the back room. The back room was reserved for those with more specialized tastes. Here the toddlers would leave one of their overall suspenders unbuttoned to indicate their special preference. An unbuttoned left suspender meant: I talk back. . . . I don't do my homework. . . . I will wet my bed until I am fifteen. . . . I will make your life a living hell. . . . You won't know what you did to deserve me. This group quickly gravitated toward the adults who carried their cigarettes in their right hands, which meant: Don't worry, we'll work it out. . . . How can I help? . . . I didn't mean it that way. . . . Where did I go wrong?

An unbuttoned right suspender meant: It was my fault. . . . I'll try to do better. . . . I cannot tell a lie. . . . I guess I'm just no good. This gang invariably found their way to the adults carrying their cigarettes in their left hands, which meant: No dessert. . . . Go to your room. . . . I threw them away. . . . *We* don't have Christmas.

As you can well imagine, a situation such as this could not go on forever. Other unnaturally inclined parents began to flock to Chicken Little. Soon they were coming in from out of town. "The weekends," said the cognoscenti, "are absolutely impossible. I mean, did you see those children in there last week? Strictly Remedial Reading, I mean really."

Finally all this activity attracted the attention of the police and late one Saturday night Chicken Little was raided. "Up against the wall, mother luckers!" shouted the cops to a group of children holding tightly to the hands of suspiciously aproned women. "Hell no, we won't grow!" the children screamed back. Suddenly a little boy broke loose from his newly acquired mother, ran to the bar, and grabbed for a bottle of milk. "Hold it right there!" yelled the officers of the law. Their warning went unheeded and the little boy was quickly joined by three other children of the sort who don't know when to stop. They all drank greedily from their respective bottles and fixed the police with impish grins, flaunting their milk mustaches. The boys in blue, pushed beyond their limits, let loose with a volley of fire. All four children were killed. And such was the tragedy of Quenched State.

Guide and Seek:
I'm O.K., You're Not

Throughout history, people have exhibited an unfortunate tendency to band together in groups. The reasons for this phenomenon vary widely but they *can* be divided into two general categories: common need and common desire. In the common need division (and I assure you that the word *common* has not been carelessly chosen) we find such things as leftish political parties, barn raisings, prides of lions, gay liberation, retirement communities, *Ms.* magazine, armies, quilting bees, the Rockettes, and est-type programs.

Under the heading of common desire—previous parenthetical comment likewise applicable—belong rightish political parties, exercise classes, the Chicago Seven, entourages, the New School for Social Research, fun crowds, and est-type programs. That some, if not all, of the particulars in each category seem to be interchangeable is due to the fact that need and desire are, like cotton madras, inclined to bleed.

The more vigilant among you may have observed that est-type programs appear in both categories. The reason for this is twofold: one, because those who participate in such programs are as desirous as they are needful, and two, because such programs are the very essence of groupness and therefore the most spectacularly unattractive. That I am totally devoid of sympathy for, or interest in, the world of groups is directly attributable to the fact that *my* two greatest needs and desires—smoking cigarettes and plotting revenge—are basically solitary pursuits. Oh, sure, sometimes a friend or two drops by and we light up together and occasionally I bounce a few vengeance ideas around with a willing companion, but actual meetings are really unnecessary.

I am therefore dismayed that programs such as est seem to be proliferating at a rate of speed traditionally associated with the more unpleasant amoebic disorders —rate of speed being only one of their shared characteristics. As this craze for personal fulfillment shows no signs of abatement, I am afraid that we shall soon be witness to programs catering to needs and desires hitherto considered overly specific. Following are a few possibilities.

rip

rip, an acronym for *r*est *i*n *p*leasure, is an organization for those deceased who feel for one reason or another that they are just not getting enough out of death. The name of the leader of this group is not known—he is, at best, an elusive figure but it is generally accepted that rip was started in response to the needs of a small coterie who often confided in one another their sporadic fears that somehow they really didn't feel *that* dead. Thus it is believed that Judge Crater, God, Amelia Earhart, Adolf Hitler, and the Lindbergh Baby are responsible for the foundation of this program.

The insecurely departed meet whenever the spirit moves them and their sessions consist largely of answering honestly a series of settling questions on the order of: "Are you saving your receipts?" "Are you coughing?" "Are you on a low-carbohydrate diet?" "Are you waiting for a check?" "Are you on hold?" "No?" responds the leader. "Then obviously you are dead. If you are dead there is no way you are not having eternal peace. If you are having eternal peace you are free from responsibility and the eventuality of being annoyed. There you have it. What could be more pleasant?"

There are certain deprivations attendant to *rip* sessions. Members are not allowed to go to the bathroom, to stretch their legs, or to eat. And although there have been no complaints from members, there are always those skeptics, those malcontents, those tearer-downers, who are convinced that were *rip* properly investigated more than one skeleton would come tumbling out of the closet.

lack

lack, or *l*outish *a*nd *c*rass *k*ollective is a program dedicated to the proposition that vulgarity and bad taste are an inalienable right. The *lackies,* as they are sometimes called, meet if they feel like it at program headquarters, which is known as La Gaucherie. La Gaucherie is densely furnished with seven thousand always-in-operation console color televisions, nine hundred constantly blaring quadrophonic stereos, shag rugs in six hundred and seventy-eight decorator colors, and an eclectic mix of Mediterranean-style dining room sets, fun sofas, interesting wall hangings, and modular seating systems. These members not otherwise occupied practicing the electric guitar or writing articles for *Playgirl* sit around in unduly comfortable positions expressing their honest feelings and opinions in loud tones of voice. Male *lackies* are encouraged to leave unbuttoned the first five buttons of their shirts unless they have unusually pale skin and hairy chests, in which case they are *required* to do so. Female members are encouraged to encourage them. Both sexes participate in a form of meditation that consists of breathing deeply of musk oil while wearing synthetic fabrics. The eventual goal of this discipline is to reach the state of mind known as Los Angeles.

hurts

hurts stands for *h*ypochondriacs *u*sually *r* *t*erribly *sick,* and sessions, which are called clinics, are held every twenty minutes in a hall known as the Waiting Room. The members file in, sit on uncomfortable leather-look couches, and read old issues of *Today's Health* until the leader, a tall, distinguished, graying-at-the-temples gentleman named Major Medical, calls the meeting to order. Members must undergo an initiation ritual, the Blood Test, before they can compare symptoms. Symptom comparison varies from session to session but all who belong to *hurts* are ever mindful of the program's motto, "There's no such thing as *just* a mole." Not infrequently the symptom comparison gets out of hand as each victim tries to outdo the other. On such occasions Major Medical finds it necessary to remind the group members of the sacred oath they took when they received the privilege of wearing the Blue Cross, and must admonish them with a painfully intoned "Patients, patients."

A World View

Departure

I board a Trans World Airlines jet to Milan the first stop on my whirlwind tour of the Continent. The plane is full of Italians (something I hadn't quite counted on). I am armed with three cartons of duty-free Vantage cigarettes and a long list of phone numbers I know I will never use. I mean I just can't see myself calling someone and saying, "Hello, you don't know me but my hair dresser occasionally sleeps with your press agent, so why don't you show me Paris." The flight is uneventful except that the gentleman to my left, a Milanese flour manufacturer wearing a green mohair suit, falls in love with me and I am compelled to spend the last three hours of the trip pretending to be in a coma.

Milan

Milan is quite an attractive little city. A nice cathedral, *The Last Supper,* a very glamorous train station built by Mussolini, la Scala, and many other enjoyable sights. There are two kinds of people in Milan. The people who work for the various *Vogue*s and the people who don't. The people who work for the various *Vogue*s are very sociable and enjoy going out. The people who don't work for the various *Vogue*s may also be very sociable but they probably don't speak much English. Almost everybody I meet in Milan is a Communist, particularly the rich. Milan is a very political place and the city is full of Communist graffiti and soldiers. Everyone in Milan is very well dressed.

In Milan you do not get matches for free. A double book of matches costs one hundred lire, which is more than fifteen cents in real money. I was appalled by this and resented it tremendously whenever anyone asked me for a light. Whenever anyone *offered* me a light I was overwhelmed by this largesse and felt that I had won something.

There is a severe change shortage in Italy. When you make a purchase that requires that the shopkeeper give you back coins he gives you candies or stamps instead. If this should happen to you, you should under no circumstances handle these stamps cavalierly. There are apparently no post offices in Italy, so if you want stamps this is your best bet. Everyone in Milan works and if it rains in Milan they blame it on Rome.

Rome

Nobody in Rome works and if it rains in Rome *and* they happen to notice it they blame it on Milan. In Rome people spend most of their time having lunch. And they do it very well—Rome is unquestionably the lunch capital of the world. Rome is very architectural and they have quite a lot of art there. The Romans are very nice people and interested in the opinions of others. As you leave the Vatican Museums you will notice to your right a suggestion box. I suggested that they put an acoustical tile ceiling in the Sistine Chapel to cut down on the incredible din produced by the German tourists. They could then reproduce all of Michelangelo's scenes in acrylic paint, thereby preserving the form *and* adding a little function.

I was in Rome for about two weeks, during which time there were five major strikes. I don't know what the strikers wanted or whether or not they got it, but it probably didn't matter. Going on strike in Rome is much more a matter of style than it is of economics. Rome is a very loony city in every respect. One needs but spend an hour or two there to realize that Fellini makes documentaries.

There is no such thing as rock and roll in Italy, so all the kids there want to be movie stars instead of heroin addicts. This is very pertinent news if you have a taste for the underaged because it means that it is possible to have an entire conversation with a fifteen-year-old without feeling as if you have to throw up.

Cannes: The Film Festival

Cannes is very cute. Lots of big white hotels, pretty beaches, starlets, yachts, lavish parties, a casino, and people who speak English. Everybody in Cannes is very busy. The producers are busy trying to get things to produce. The directors are busy trying to get things to direct. The buyers are busy trying to get sellers. The sellers are busy trying to get buyers. And the waiters are busy trying not to take your order. The best way to meet people in Cannes is to sit on the Carleton Terrace and order a drink. A few hours later the waiter will bring you somebody else's martini. You pick up the martini in an extravagant manner and look around. A few tables away someone will be holding your Perrier with a twist in a quizzical position and you will be well on your way to making a friend and/or deal.

There are about two hundred films a day shown in Cannes. I saw two and a half. It costs a lot of money to get to France and I can go to the movies in New York. Anyway, you know what they say about screening rooms —in the dark they all look alike.

Paris

Paris is a great beauty. As such it possesses all the qualities that one finds in any other great beauty: chic, sexiness, grandeur, arrogance, and the absolute inability and refusal to listen to reason. So if you're going there you would do well to remember this: no matter how politely or distinctly you ask a Parisian a question he will persist in answering you in French.

Notes on "Trick"

trick, *n.* from OFr. *trichier,* to trick, to cheat; Pr. *tric,* deceit; *It. treccare,* to cheat. 1. an action or device designed to deceive, swindle, etc.; artifice; a dodge; ruse; stratagem; deception. 2. a practical joke; a mischievous or playful act; prank. . . . 4. (a) a clever or difficult act intended to amuse . . . (b) any feat requiring skill. 5. the art, method, or process of doing something successfully or of getting a result quickly . . . 6. an expedient or convention of an art, craft, or trade . . . 7. a personal mannerism . . .

I have chosen these definitions, carefully selected from the Unabridged Second Edition of Webster's Dictionary, on the basis of congeniality with what is perhaps the most current usage of the word *Trick*—that which refers to the object of one's affectations. By "one" I mean the person of serious ambition in those fields most likely to necessitate the employment of a press agent. Such a person is often, but not always, a homosexual; the primary reason for this being that the heterosexual is far too burdened by his own young to be much interested in anyone else's. Where the heterosexual feels a sense of duty, a sense of honor, a sense of responsibility, the homosexual feels a sense of humor, a sense of protocol, and most significantly, a sense of design.

With no dependents, he is free to pursue his selfish interests—among these, the Trick. The Trick allows one a semblance of romantic intimacy without the risk that one's own importance will be improperly appreciated.

The Trick exhibits those qualities found in a favorite toy. Surely, no sane person would if he could help it knowingly choose a doll that talked about progressive education and demanded that one share the housework —and it is precisely this ability to help it that separates the men from the toys.

Fortunately, there are many available to fill the role of Trick, since the first requirement of the climber is a toehold. In allowing this close proximity one is, indeed, apt to have one's pocket picked, but one also has the option of causing a nasty spill. It is, therefore, a situation in which everyone concerned can be taken advantage of to the best of his ability. As to the question of who runs the greatest risk of getting hurt, one can only reply that the number of mountains that have suffered severe or fatal injury is inflnitesimal when compared to the number who have tackled them.

The word Trick is used to describe the less illustrious member of such an alliance and it fills a genuine need. For the noteworthy partner the words Rich and/or Famous are quite sufficient, but the corresponding adjectives of Cute and/or Well-built are somewhat lacking. Actual names were all right for home use, but neither "Juan" nor "Heather" is really serviceable as a generic term.

Exactly when or why the word Trick was first used for this purpose is unclear, although there is a theory that it derives from the slang of prostitutes, who have long used it in regard to their clients. While this contention is not without logic it is far more likely that this use of the word Trick was spread by simple (or complex) word of mouth.

I have in the interest of clarification jotted down some notes on the subject, but before we proceed to them there are a few things that must be said:

Tricks like to lie in bed—also in restaurants.

* * *

Tricks should never be left strewn carelessly about the house where someone might trip over them.

* * *

Tricks are attracted to bright objects. This may elude your understanding since you obviously do not share this tendency.

These notes are for Lord Alfred Douglas.

1. It is wise to avoid the very young Trick. For while it is indeed true that they offer the advantage of having to leave early to get to school, it is equally true that the very same thing can be accomplished by the use of fashion models, who will not only have to be standing on top of the Pan Am Building in full makeup by 8 A.M. but who also will never need help with their term papers on John Donne.

2. The homosexual's desire to remain youthful is entirely based on his knowledge that he will never have children and hence will be deprived of legitimately meeting their more attractive friends.

3. There are those for whom the most highly prized quality in a Trick is sheer stupidity. Of this group the most envied is an eminent film director who has installed in his residence a young man whose lips move when he watches television.

4. Random examples of items that are part of the canon of Trick:

Bennington College's Nonresident Term
Conceptual art
Stealing
Trying on someone else's leather jacket while he's at
  work
Artistic greeting cards
Interesting food
Black sheets
Remembering telephone numbers by making a word
  out of the corresponding letters
Trying to figure things out by listening to the lyrics of
  popular songs
Exotic cigarettes
Reading, or more likely watching, *Breakfast at
  Tiffany's* and identifying with Holly Golightly
Hearing about F. Scott Fitzgerald and thinking you're
  Zelda
Being Zelda Fitzgerald and thinking you're F. Scott
Lina Wertmüller movies seen without nausea
Stag movies seen with lust

5. A good Trick, like a good child, is mannerly. He
does not speak unless spoken to, he does not contradict,
and he kneels when an adult comes into the room.

> "Still as interested as ever in the young, I see," Francis
> remarked in a confidential undertone, glancing round the
> obstruction of his friend's shoulders to where Daniel
> stood. . . . "You old succubus! Let's have a look at your
> latest suffix!"
>
> —*The Apes of God,*
> Wyndham Lewis

6. Mixed company in the modern sense of the term
means that Tricks are present. How often one has
longed to be left alone after dinner while the Tricks go
upstairs and take cocaine.

7. American industry has made a grave error in
overlooking the Trick. The market is wide open and
would be rewardingly receptive to such products as

strawberry-swirl vodka, Hermès mittens, and a pack of cigarettes with a secret surprise inside.

8. Although the male Trick is more prone to stealing than is the female, neither sex can be trusted alone in the same room with an invitation to a party at Halston's.

9. Tricks have feelings too, as they will be the first to tell you. If you prick them they do indeed bleed—usually your good vodka.

10. The Trick is, when it comes to finance, truly a child of the modern age, for he never carries cash—at least not his own.

11. Other people's Tricks pose a special problem. Upon coming across a friend thus accompanied you must, out of politeness, treat the Trick amicably. This is invariably a mistake, for shortly thereafter the friend will divest himself of his consort and for the rest of your life the Trick will be coming up to you at parties and saying hello.

12. The simple black Trick is always appropriate—particularly at events where food is not served.

13. It is not unusual for the male aficionado to draw his Tricks exclusively from the lower orders. Such a person is, indeed, often attracted to the criminal element. When asked wherein lay the appeal, a spokesman for this group replied, "Everybody looks good when they're under arrest."

"Horace has always been like that—his intentions have *always* been strictly honourable" sneered Ratner "and he has never lost his belief in 'genius'—associated *always* with extreme youth, and a pretty face! Unfortunately, the type of beauty which appeals to Horace you see is rather commonplace. The result is Horace has never actually met with a 'genius,' which is a pity. It might have opened his eyes if he had!"

—*The Apes of God,*
Wyndham Lewis

14. Should you be awakened in the middle of the night by a faint scratching sound, do not fear for your health unless you are certain that all valuables have been safely locked away. For it is far less likely that your Trick is suffering a communicable rash than that he is copying out your address book. The more vindictive among you may be interested in devising a phony version of said book in which you have carefully set down the phone numbers of particularly vile ex-Tricks next to the names of your most prestigious and least favorite former employers.

15. The mistreatment of Tricks is the revenge of the intelligent upon the beautiful.

16. Regrettably few Tricks are attractive enough to be allowed to discuss their innermost thoughts. Only those possessed of truly incredible cheekbones should ever be permitted to use the word *energy* in a sentence unless they are referring to heating oil.

17. The Trick is not an equal but he is often an equalizer.

18. Occasionally a Trick will succeed so spectacularly that he will make the transition to person. When this occurs he will assume a truly amazing imperiousness of manner. People love to feel superior to their past.

19. Tricks almost always have pets. This is understandable, as everyone needs someone they can talk to on their own level.

20. Taking an emergency telephone call from a Dr. Juan or a Dr. Heather is certain to result in overinvolvement.

21. There is a distinct Trick taste in literature. Among favorite Trick books are those dealing with the quest for God, such as the words of Carlos Castaneda and Herman Hesse; those depicting a glamorous and torturous homosexuality, as in the case of *Nightwood* by Djuna Barnes; and those assuring Tricks that everything is fine and dandy, especially them. This sort of reading is generally

harmless providing they have mastered the technique of reading quietly to themselves. For even the most hopelessly smitten will bridle at being awakened by Anaïs Nin.

22. When it comes to the visual arts a marked Trick preference is also evident. Work that falls into this category is easy to recognize, as the Trick is unfailingly attracted to that which looks as if he could (or did) make it himself.

23. Art movies on television are ideal for luring the reluctant Trick to one's apartment. There are very few people who dabble in this field who have not seen the first twenty minutes of *Loves of a Blonde* more times than they care to count.

24. The Trick is, without fail, drawn to the interesting job. Interesting jobs, in this sense, include not only work in museum gift shops but also minor positions on the production crews of documentary films concerning birth defects.

25. The Trick, more often than not, will display an unconquerable bent for creativity. The East Coast Trick leans heavily toward the composition of free-verse poetry, while his West Coast counterpart goes in for songwriting. Tricks of all regions own expensive cameras with which they take swaggeringly grainy photographs of nearby planets and sensitive young drug addicts. This is not difficult to understand, as they are relentless admirers of that which they call art and you call hobbies.

> "Can't you see Dan that you are Horace's plaything—
> When he talks about your 'genius'—pulling your leg—
> that's to get your 'genius'!—*People always pull other people's legs when they want to get hold of their genius!*
>
> —*The Apes of God,*
> Wyndham Lewis

26. One man's Trick is another man's design assistant.
27. A New York hostess with a penchant for young

boys gave a dinner at which a kind and fatherly magazine editor found himself seated across from her Trick. Seeking to put the boy at ease, the editor asked him politely what he did. "I'm an alchemist," the boy replied. Overhearing the exchange, another guest whispered, "Alchemist? They *used* to be bank clerks."

28. There is occasionally some question as to which member of a given duo *is* the Trick. This sort of confusion results when one (the elder) has money and the other (the younger) has talent. In such cases, and with all due respect to rising young luminaries, unless the money is exceedingly new and the talent exceedingly large, the money, as is its wont, wins. Or as was once said to a somewhat braggardly young artist while window-shopping at Porthaults, "If she has *those* sheets, you're the Trick."

29. Tricks like you for what they aren't. You like Tricks for what you haven't.

30. If one half of the couple is a waiter or waitress, he or she is always the Trick. Particularly, or in the case of New York City inevitably, if he or she has artistic ambitions. Such individuals may indeed traffic with those that they in turn refer to as Tricks, but that is a level of society far too submerged to be of any interest.

31. At public gatherings Tricks have been observed speaking to one another. What they actually say can only be a matter of conjecture but it is safe to assume that no money is changing hands.

32. The female Trick of great beauty can be readily identified by her habit of putting a cigarette in her mouth with an attitude of absolute assurance that someone else will light it.

33. It might appear to the casual observer that wives are Tricks. This betrays a sorry lack of perception, since no word as innately lighthearted as Trick could ever be used to describe someone with whom you share a joint checking account.

34. It is not good form to take a Trick out unless one

is so firmly established as to be able to afford being associated with someone who might at any given moment write a poem in public.

35. Tricks are often plenteous gift givers. Upon receiving such offerings, one does well to forget old adages, for while it may certainly be true that good things come in small packages it must not be forgotten that this is also the case with ceramic jewelry.

36. Letters from female Tricks are immediately recognizable, as these girls are greatly inclined to cross their sevens and dot their *i*'s with little circles. In all probability this is caused by their associating the presence of a writing implement in their hand with the playing of tic-tac-toe.

> "There is a Talmudic saying," smiled Dr. Frumpfausen . . . "as follows. In choosing a friend, ascend a step. In choosing a wife, descend a step. When Froggie-would-a-wooing-go, when Froggie is you, my dear boy, he must step *down,* as many steps as there are beneath him—even unto the last! . . ."
>
> —*The Apes of God,*
> Wyndham Lewis

37. Tricks are distinctly susceptible to the allure of faraway places. If you reside in the Village they want to breakfast at the Plaza. If you live in Murray Hill it's Chinatown they long for. But no matter where you make your home, they all share a consuming desire to ride, in the middle of the night, the Staten Island Ferry. They will, without exception, consider your rejection of such a proposal cold and unfeeling, little realizing that you are simply protecting them from what you know would be overwhelming temptation were you ever to find yourself standing behind them on a moving boat.

Science

Science

Science is not a pretty thing. It is unpleasantly proportioned, outlandishly attired, and often overeager. What, then, is the appeal of science? What accounts for its popularity? And who gave it its start?

In order to better understand the modern penchant for science it is necessary to take the historical point of view. Upon doing this, one makes the discovery that the further back one goes the less science one is likely to find. And that the science one does encounter is of a consistently higher quality. For example, in studying the science of yesteryear one comes upon such interesting notions as gravity, electricity, and the roundness of the earth—while an examination of more recent phenomena shows a strong trend toward spray cheese, stretch denim, and the Moog synthesizer.

These data unquestionably support my theory that modern science was largely conceived of as an answer to the servant problem and that it is generally practiced by those who lack a flair for conversation.

It is therefore not surprising that only after Abolition did science begin to display its most unsavory features.

Inventions and discoveries became progressively less desirable as it became harder and harder to get good help.

Prior to the advent of this unfortunate situation the scientist was chiefly concerned with the theoretical. His needs properly attended to, he quite rightly saw no reason to disturb others by finding a practical application for his newfound knowledge. This resulted in the establishment of schools of thought rather than schools of computer programming. That this was a much pleasanter state of affairs than presently exists is indisputable, and one has only to look around to see that the unseemliness of modern science is basically the product of men whose peevish reactions to household disorder drove them to folly. Even in those cases where a practical touch was indicated one notes a tendency toward excess.

A typical example of this syndrome is Thomas Edison. Edison invented the electric light bulb, the purpose of which was to make it possible for one to read at night. A great and admirable achievement and one that would undoubtedly have earned him a permanent place in the hearts and minds of civilized men had he not then turned around and invented the phonograph. This single act led to the eventual furnishing of small apartments with quadrophonic sound systems, thereby making it impossible for the better element to properly enjoy his *good* invention. If one follows this line of thought to its logical conclusion one clearly sees that almost without exception every displeasing aspect of science is, in one way or another, a hideous corruption of the concept of reading at night. Reading is not a particularly popular pastime—hence the warm welcome the majority of the population has extended to such things as snowmobiles, tape decks, and citizen band radios. That these newer appliances have not entirely taken away the appetite of the public for electric lamps can only be attributed to their unwillingness to let perfectly good empty sangria bottles go to waste.

Scientists are rarely to be counted among the fun people. Awkward at parties, shy with strangers, deficient in irony—they have had no choice but to turn their attention to the close study of everyday objects. They have had ample opportunity to do so and on occasion have been rewarded with gratifying insights.

Thus electricity was the product of Franklin's interest in lightning, the concept of gravity the outcome of Newton's experience with an apple, and the steam engine the result of Watt's observation of a teakettle.

It is only to be expected that people of this sort are not often invited out. After all, a person who might well spend an entire evening staring at a kitchen utensil has little to recommend him as a dinner companion. It is far too risky—particularly if the person in question is moved to share his thoughts with others. Physical laws are not amusing. Mathematical symbols do not readily lend themselves to the double entendre. Chemical properties are seldom cause for levity. These facts make it intolerable for a gathering ever to include more than one scientist. If it is unavoidable, a scientist may be safely invited to dinner providing that he is absolutely the only member of his profession present. More than one scientist at the table is bad luck—not to mention bad taste. Legend has it that the atom was split when a bunch of scientists working late decided to order in a pizza. Indeed a terrifying story and one made all the more chilling when one learns that a number of their colleagues smarting from the snub of being excluded from this impromptu meal spitefully repaired to an all-night diner and invented polyester.

The Nail Bank:
Not Just Another Clip Joint

During a recent luncheon with a practicing member of the leisure class the subject of fingernail care chanced (as it so often does) to come up. My companion chided me for what she considered to be the disgraceful condition of my fingernails and suggested quite strongly that I accompany her to the inordinately tony establishment that is responsible for the impeccable condition of her own. Upon learning the cost of such an outing I curled my upper lip in an attractive yet forceful manner and declined her invitation with little regret. I was, however, helpless against the demands of my constantly questing mind and felt compelled to inquire as to what exactly could be done to fingernails to warrant such expense. "Why," replied my friend, "they shape them, they wrap them, they polish them, and if I need it they give me a transplant." "A transplant," I repeated. "What do you mean, a transplant?"

"Well, if I break a nail and I have the broken piece they put it back on. But if I don't they use someone else's nail from the nail bank." "The nail bank?" I repeated again.

"Yes," she said and began to explain further, but I must confess that I was no longer listening, for I was far too intent on my own imaginings. I left the table in a daze and remember little of the hours that followed, since my mind was reeling with vivid nail bank visions. I have finally managed to get some sort of grip on this thing and here is how it works:

Every year there is a nail drive. Volunteer nail workers set up shop in such likely establishments as finishing schools, health clubs, secretarial pools, and Henri Bendel's. The donor enters the room set aside for this purpose, lies down on a portable Ultrasuede chaise longue, and extends her hands. The volunteer nail worker carefully clips three nails from each hand (any more would be dangerous; any less, uncharitable) and then offers the donor a glass of Knox gelatine so that she may regain her strength. The nails are then placed in sterile containers and rushed to the nail bank. There they are typed accordingly:

Type O—Oval
Type A—Angular
Type B—Bent, slightly
Rh negative—Right hand, out of the question

When the victim of a broken nail is brought into the salon a team of dedicated manicurists matches the victim's type with the specimens on hand and performs the transplant with meticulous skill. There are, however, frequent shortages and it is not uncommon for a victim to wait days for a compatible type. Measures, of course, have been taken to alleviate this situation. During the annual nail drive volunteers comb the city in an effort to convince those girls too selfish to donate in life to do so in death. These girls carry upon their persons cards that in the event of their demise instruct the authorities to clip so that another might receive the gift of renewed length. When one of these girls meets with a fatal accident that miraculously leaves her nails intact, a manicurist is raced to the scene and the procedure is carried out with dignity and dispatch.

Now, it sometimes happens that there are two girls in need of the same type nail but only one such nail is available. In a case like this the nail properly goes to the better tipper, but occasionally both girls are equally matched in this department. When this occurs the girls are brought before a judicial body known formally as the Emery Board. The Emery Board is composed of four experts in the field: a hairdresser, a headwaiter, a doorman, and Another Woman. The board members ask the girls the following pertinent questions:

1. Where are you going this evening?
2. With whom?
3. Wearing what?

The girls are then asked to leave the room while the judges confer. More often than not a decision is reached based upon the answers to the board's questions, but from time to time there is a deadlock. In such a circumstance the girls are not without recourse, for they can then turn to the Court of Appeal. The Court of Appeal is presided over by a temperamental photographer and a dictatorial fashion editor. The Court of Appeal is a visual rather than a verbal institution and favorable judgments are awarded solely on the basis of polish. Decisions of the Court of Appeal are final. Recently, however, it was discovered that the judges had ruled against a girl who lived on Beekman Place in favor of one who resided in the West Seventies. The judges were understandably relieved when this decision was overturned, for they, too, are firm believers in that wise old adage: Nothing succeeds like address.

Digital Clocks and
Pocket Calculators:
Spoilers of Youth

I was in certain respects a rather precocious youngster. My glance, right from the start, was fraught with significance and I was unquestionably the first child on my block to use the word *indisposed* in a sentence. My childhood was not, however, quite the gay whirl that one might imagine from the above statements. As a whistler I was only fair and I am to this very day unable to assume even a humane attitude in regard to gerbils. But then as now, I was always capable of dealing with the larger issues—it was, and is, the little things that get me down.

I did not learn how to tell time until I was nine years old. This is an unusually advanced age at which to master the art, except perhaps in Southern California.

My parents were understandably upset about my inability to tell time, for they possessed the foresight to realize that any child who talked back with such verve and snap would one day need a lawyer who charged by the hour. Furthermore, their infinite wisdom told them that it was exceedingly unlikely that the bill would arrive reading: Consultation on contract with agent,

$150.00. One and one-half hours. From big hand on twelve, little hand on three, to little hand on four, big hand on six.

Their concern for my future well-being drove them to frantic efforts in an attempt to instill in me the knowledge that so painfully eluded my grasp. Night after night I sat at the kitchen table and surveyed a bewildering array of clocks made from oatmeal cookies, peanut butter lids, and crayoned circles of colored paper. They spelled each other—first one parent and then the other —taking turns on watch, so to speak. They were diligent, patient, and kind and I nodded my head and looked alert, all the while seething with fury at the injustices of a world in which we didn't have Christmas but we did have Time. As the days wore on and my ignorance persisted, my parents toyed with the idea of renting me out as a parlor game or at least trading me in for a child who couldn't learn something else—so weary were they of round, flattish objects.

Outside intervention came in the form of an offer of help from my aunt to take me on for the week of my winter vacation. I was duly dispatched to Poughkeepsie, where I was alternately bribed with banana milk shakes and tortured with clocks devised from paper plates, circular throw pillows, and overturned frying pans. At the end of the week I was returned to my parents a thing that was once a child—as ever unable to tell time and newly addicted to banana milk shakes in a household that considered blenders frivolous.

Some months later I was taking a bath when I suddenly shouted "Eureka!" and at long last such concepts as twenty of eight and ten after twelve were touched with meaning.

It should be readily apparent to all that under no circumstances will I ever consider yielding the need for such hard-won knowledge. That there does indeed exist the very real danger of such a possibility is entirely due to the invention of the digital clock. I spent the best years of my life learning to tell time and I'm not stopping now. Neither should you. Here's why:

1. Regular clocks tell real time. Real time is time such as half-past seven.
2. Digital clocks tell fake time. Fake time is time such a nine-seventeen.
3. Nine-seventeen is fake time because the only people who ever have to know that it's nine-seventeen are men who drive subway trains.
4. I am not a man who drives a subway train.
5. You are not a man who drives a subway train.
6. I can tell this without even seeing you because anyone who has to know that it's nine-seventeen cannot possibly risk looking away.
7. Real watch faces are in the shape of watch faces because they must accommodate all of the things that make up a real watch, such as numbers, hands, and little minute lines.
8. Digital watch faces are in the shape of watch faces for no apparent reason. This cannot help but have an unsettling effect upon the young.

Now that I have set the record straight on the matter of Time I should like to direct your attention briefly to another unacceptable invention:

Pocket Calculators: It Took Me Three Years to Learn How to Do Long Division and So Should They

1. The rigors of learning how to do long division have been a traditional part of childhood, just like learning to smoke. In fact, as far as I am concerned, the two go hand in hand. Any child who cannot do long division by himself does not deserve to smoke. I am really quite a nice girl and very fond of children but I do have my standards. I have never taught a child to smoke before he has first taken a piece of paper and a pencil and demonstrated to my satisfaction that he can correctly divide 163 by 12.

2. Pocket calculators are not inexpensive and, generally speaking, parents would be better off spending
the money on themselves. If they *must* throw it away
on their offspring they would do well to keep in mind
that a pack of cigarettes rarely costs more than sev-
enty-five cents.

3. It is unnatural for *anyone,* let alone a *child,* to be
able under any circumstances whatsoever to divide
17.3 by 945.8.

4. Pocket calculators encourage children to think that
they have all the answers. If this belief were actually
to take hold they might well seize power, which
would undoubtedly result in all of the furniture
being much too small.

A Final Word

I am not personally a parent. But I do have two god-
children and am expecting a third. I am naturally concerned for their future. If I ruled the world you could bet
your boots that none of them would ever set their eyes
on any such contraptions as digital clocks and pocket
calculators. But alas, I do not rule the world and that, I
am afraid, is the story of my life—always a godmother,
never a God.

Weak Speech Handsets: Aid for the Dull

The average person reacts to the arrival of his phone bill with a simple snort of disgust, but I frequently find my displeasure tempered with a touch of anticipation. For, unpleasant as it is to receive the written proof that one has indeed been whiling away the slender remainder of one's youth in costly, idle chat, one is nevertheless helpless against the fact that one is inordinately fond of a good long read. And quite fortunate that is; for the phone bills that I receive are not the sort of phone bills one glances at—they are the sort of phone bills one leafs through.

While recently perusing such a document my attention was immediately captured by two rather jarring particulars. The first being that although I had spent the lion's share of the month not at home, my bill was thick with calls to expensive parts of the nation. I mulled this over and decided that this irregularity could be easily explained if one was willing to accept the possibility that a heroin addict well connected in the movie business had periodically broken into my apartment and called Beverly Hills. I accepted, without reservation, just such a possibility. The second attention-getter was an item that appeared on the back of page eight, where I discovered a list of special phones available to the discriminating caller:

1. Trimline
2. Princess
3. Bell Chime
4. Tone Ringer
5. Volume Control Handset
6. Weak Speech Handset

I had a brief flirtation with Bell Chime and a frivolous dalliance with Tone Ringer, but my heart was won by Weak Speech Handset.

I considered momentarily the possibility that the Weak Speech Handset had been designed for those who had suffered some unfortunate incident of the throat but quickly discarded the notion that the phone company was capable of such realism. I cast about for a likely theory and hit upon the following.

The Weak Speech Handset is aimed at the tedious crowd—those who are weak in the speech department. This device takes the wearisome remarks of the boring and converts them into sparkling repartee. There is no question but that such an invention is long overdue. It is, however, quite unlikely that its usefulness will be much recognized by those who need it most. It is probable, then, that Weak Speech Handsets will be largely purchased as gifts. And perhaps therein lies a certain justice; undoubtedly the listener will derive the greatest benefits. For one cannot help but assume that if the caller was as aware of his ennui-inducing qualities as was the callee, he would stop talking entirely and concentrate on his personal appearance.

Believing strongly that variety is the spice of life, I have thoughtfully prepared a catalog detailing a wide selection of models from which to choose.

The Oscar Wilde

Produces speech that is entirely epigrammatic. . . . You will fool no one, but in certain small sections of the country you will be very popular . . . in certain other sections of the country you will be arrested. . . . A great favorite among consenting adults . . . available only in yellow.

The Dorothy Parker

A sarcasm lover's delight . . . particularly efficient at making humorous remarks on the subject of suicide. . . . Order now and receive as a free bonus an attractive round table.

The Gore Vidal

A bit higher priced but you will profit in hours of rib-tickling fun. . . . Fully equipped with self-transformer. . . . dispenses once and for all with the need for two phones . . . perfect for Him *and* Her.

The Evelyn Waugh

Thrill and amaze your loved one . . . the ultimate in contempt . . . a must for those with a taste for the trenchant.

The Alexander Pope

A sure-fire hit with heroic-couplet buffs . . . especially entertaining in matters pertaining to hair.

The Primary Cause
of Heterosexuality
Among Males in Urban Areas:
Yet Another Crackpot Theory

The most commonly heard complaint among heterosexual women in New York concerns the dearth of heterosexual men. Should you hear such talk you would be well advised to direct the complainant to a Soho bar. For here she would be surrounded by such a plethora of eager gents that she might well wonder just who's buying all those plaid flannel shirts. Why, she may ask, is this particular quarter of the city so heavily populated by young men to whom the name Ronald Firbank means nothing? To this query there can be only one reply—heterosexuality among males in urban areas is caused primarily by overcrowding in artist colonies. This is a scientific fact. Here is how we know.

Scientists observed over a long period of time the behavior of a group of twenty rats living in an apartment with high ceilings and working fireplaces. All twenty rats were artists. All twenty rats were, as is normal in such cases, homosexual. Five of these rats were chosen at random and taken in a knapsack to West Broadway, where they were moved into a loft. They were joined there by ninety-five other rats who were also homosexual artists and had also been chosen at random from a number of other natural habitats such as doorman buildings and converted brownstones. All hundred rats had, when in their proper environments, exhibited absolutely no inclination toward unusual sexual behavior. Once, however, faced with life in a neighborhood that contained so many galleries and so few decent restaurants, an alarming pattern began to emerge. First they stopped painting and started having concepts. Then they began consuming a diet heavy in raisins and the less expensive but heartier red wines. Finally, many of them displayed a decided tendency to teach two days a week at the School of Visual Arts. Once this occurred they were past the point of no return and began seeking the company of female rats who had gone to Bennington in the late sixties.

The scientists, understandably horrified by the results of their tampering with the natural order, tried to stem the rising tide of heterosexuality by appealing to the rats' greatest weakness. They chose a small group of rats who had previously been the most hard-core of the S & M crowd. They led them over to the docks on the Hudson River. Here they attempted to stir old fires by tossing into the murky waters those accoutrements most cherished before the move to Soho. First they let dangle and then drop a black leather cap with metal ornaments. The rats responded with agitated tail movements but stayed put. Next they tried a pair of rugged boots complete with menacing-looking spurs. Still no action. Finally the scientists threw into the river a long, snaky leather whip. Their spirits lifted as several of the rats scurried to the edge of the dock. But instinct was overcome by conditioning, and they watched with heavy hearts and defeated eyes the rats desert the sinking whip.

Why I Love Sleep

I love sleep because it is both pleasant and safe to use. Pleasant because one is in the best possible company and safe because sleep is the consummate protection against the unseemliness that is the invariable consequence of being awake. What you don't know won't hurt you. Sleep is death without the responsibility.

The danger, of course, is that sleep appears to be rather addictive. Many find that they cannot do without it and will go to great lengths to ensure its possession. Such people have been known to neglect home, hearth, and even publishers' deadlines in the crazed pursuit of their objective. I must confess that I, too, am a sleeper and until quite recently was riddled with guilt because of it. But then I considered the subject more carefully and what I learned not only relieved my guilt but also made me proud to be among the fatigued.

I would like to share my findings so that others might feel free to lay down their once uplifted heads. I have therefore prepared a brief course of instruction in order to instill pride in those who sleep.

The Fran Lebowitz Sleep Studies Program

Sleep is a genetic rather than an acquired trait. If your parents were sleepers, chances are that you will be too. This is not cause for despair but rather for pride in a heritage that you share not only with your family but also with a fine group of well-known historical figures. The following list is indicative of the diversity to be found among sleepers:

Some Well-known Historical Figures Who Were Sleepers

Dwight D. Eisenhower

While many remember Ike (as he was affectionately called by an adoring nation) for his golf, there is little doubt but that he was a sleeper from childhood, a trait he unquestionably carried with him to the White House. In fact, so strongly committed was he to sleep that one could barely distinguish Ike's sleeping from Ike's waking.

William Shakespeare

Known as the Bard among his colleagues in the word game, Shakespeare was undoubtedly one of literature's most inspired and prolific sleepers. Proof of this exists in the form of a bed found in the house he occupied in Stratford-upon-Avon. Further references to sleeping have been discovered in his work, and although there is some question as to whether he actually did all his own sleeping (scholarly debate currently centers around the possibility that some of it was done by Sir Francis Bacon), we are nevertheless safe in assuming that William Shakespeare was indeed a sleeper of note.

e. e. cummings

The evidence that e. e. cummings was a sleeper is admittedly sparse. Therefore, it is generally accepted that he was perhaps more of a napper.

It is only to be expected that if so many well-known historical figures were sleepers, their accomplishments should be of equal import. Following is a partial list of such achievements:

Some Contributions to World Culture Made by Sleepers

> Architecture
> Language
> Science
> The wheel
> Fire

I rest my case.

Good Weather
and Its Propensity to Frequent
the Better Neighborhoods

It was once the common belief that the climate was determined by a large number of gods, each in charge of a specific variety of weather. Then came the major religions, and most people came to hold a more subdued point of view that suggested but a single god who got around a lot. Many still take this position, although the majority now ascribe to a theory of weather based largely on cloud formation, air pressure, wind velocity, and other aspects of science. Lastly, there are those who feel that the weather and what it does are entirely the province of honey-throated television announcers with big Magic Markers. So, then, we are presented with three basic theories as regards the controlling factor of weather:

    A. God
    B. Nature
    C. Tone of Voice

To the casual observer it would appear that these three theories are widely disparate. That, of course, is

the problem with casual observers. Their very casual-
ness—that trait we once all found so attractive . . . so
appealing . . . so devil-may-care—is precisely what
makes them so quick to judge and therefore so frequently inaccurate. The more vigilant observer would
unquestioningly be able to detect a rather striking
similarity. That similarity being that all three theories
are based quite simply on mere whim—God can change
his mind, Nature can change her course, and Voice, as
we all know only too well, can change its tone.

Thus we find that by and large the world considers
weather to be something, if not all, of a romantic—given
to dashing about hither and yon raining and snowing
and cooling and heating with a capriciousness astonish-
ing if not downright ridiculous in one so mature. Well,
the world may think what it bloody well likes but I for
one will have nothing to do with such faulty logic and
so have formulated what I believe to be a more reasonable theory.

"Why," I asked myself, "should the weather be any
different from you or me—are we not all one?" When
presented with a question of such startling clarity I was
compelled to answer, "No reason, Fran, no reason at
all." "Well then," I continued, "it follows that if weather
is no different from you or me, then it must be the same
as you or me, in which case that which controls *us* must
control *it*." "Can't argue with that," I replied, realizing
with a start that I was in the presence of a master. "And
what," I queried further, "do you think that is? Only one
thing—money. That's right, money." "When you're
right you're right," was the welcome reply, and with
that my companion and I strode off happily hand in
hand—a gesture which, while it did lend us a certain
September Mornish aspect, was in no way unattractive.

While some may find this argument specious, I offer
the following as absolute definitive evidence that it is
money and money alone that influences the weather.

1. On August 13, 1975, at 3:00 P.M., the temperature on Fourteenth Street and Eighth Avenue was ninety-four degrees—the humidity 85 percent. On the exact same date and at the exact same time the temperature on Seventy-third Street and Fifth Avenue was a balmy seventy-one degrees—the humidity a comfortable 40 percent. I know, because I was there.

2. The only recorded instance of rain on Sutton Place occurred when a scene from a big-budget movie was being shot in the vicinity and the script called for inclement weather. The moment the powerful Hollywood director yelled "Cut!" the rain stopped.

3. The reason that then mayor John Lindsay did not send snowplows to Queens during that much publicized blizzard was that he lived on Gracie Square, where on the day in question he was lying on his terrace taking the sun.

4. It is widely believed that in the summer rich people leave New York to go to Southampton because the weather is cooler there. This is not true. What actually happens is that in the summer the cooler weather leaves New York and goes to Southampton because it doesn't want to stay in New York with a lot of underpaid writers and Puerto Ricans.

5. Generally speaking, the weather is better on the East Side than on the West Side. All in all, the weather considered this arrangement satisfactory except for the problem posed by the better buildings on Central Park West. The problem was solved by means of a trade-off with certain buildings in the East Seventies that are largely populated by beyond-their-means airline stewardesses and the proprietors of leather boutiques. Thus the San Remo and the Dakota receive weather appropriate to their architecture and airline stewardesses and the proprietors of leather boutiques are perhaps those among us who most fully understand the meaning of the term "fair-weather friend."

Plants:
The Roots of All Evil

The Unabridged Second Edition of Webster's Dictionary—a volume of no small repute—gives the following as the second definition of the word *plant:* "any living thing that cannot move voluntarily, has no sense organs and generally makes its own food. . . ." I have chosen the second definition in favor of the first because it better serves my purpose, which is to prove once and for all that, except in extremely rare instances, a plant is really not the sort of thing that one ought to have around the house. That this might be accomplished in an orderly manner, I have elected to consider each aspect of the above definition individually. Let us begin at the beginning:

Any Living Thing

In furnishing one's place of residence one seeks to acquire those things which will provide the utmost in beauty, comfort, and usefulness. In the beauty department one is invariably drawn to such fixtures as Cocteau drawings, Ming vases, and Aubusson rugs. Comfort is, of course, assured by the ability to possess these objects. Usefulness is something best left to those trained in such matters.

It should, then, be apparent that at no time does Any Living Thing enter the picture except in the past tense. In other words, it is perfectly acceptable to surround oneself with objects composed of that which while alive may have been Any Living Thing but in death has achieved dignity by becoming a nice white linen sheet.

That Cannot Move Voluntarily

Here one is confronted with the problem that arises when Any Living Thing takes the form of an extra person. An extra person is quite simply a person other than oneself. Living things of this nature undoubtedly have their place in both town and country, as they usually prove to be the most adept at typing, kissing, and conversing in an amusing fashion. It must be pointed out, however, that moving voluntarily is the very key to their success in performing these functions; the necessity of having to actually operate them would quite eliminate their appeal.

I have previously stated my contention that plants are acceptable in extremely rare instances. This type of extremely rare instance occurs when one is presented with a leaf-ridden token of affection by an extra person who has provided valuable service. Refusal of a plant thus offered will almost certainly result in the termination of this bond. Therefore, while the decision as to who exactly should be allowed to burden one with such a memento is, of course, a matter of personal conscience, one is wise to remember that talk is cheap, a kiss is just a kiss, but manuscripts do not type themselves.

Has No Sense Organs

It is necessary to remember that, although No Sense Organs does most assuredly guarantee no meaningful glances, no snorting derisively, and no little tastes, it also, alas, guarantees no listening spellbound.

And Generally Makes Its Own Food

There is, I believe, something just the tiniest bit smug in that statement. And Generally Makes Its Own Food, does it? Well, bully for It. I do not generally make my own food, nor do I apologize for it in the least. New York City is fairly bristling with restaurants of every description and I cannot help but assume that they are there for a reason. Furthermore, it is hard to cherish the notion of a cuisine based on photosynthesis. Thus, since I have yet to detect the aroma of Fettuccine Alfredo emanating from a Boston fern, I do not consider And Generally Makes Its Own Food to be a trait of any consequence whatsoever. When you run across one that Generally Makes Its Own Money, give me a call.

Mars:
Living in a Small Way

Not too long ago the United States succeeded in landing on Mars an unmanned spacecraft, the chief purpose of which was to ascertain whether or not anyone lives there. The results are not all in yet but there is, I am afraid, little doubt that the answer will be in the affirmative. It is pointless to assume that the earth alone is afflicted with the phenomenon of life.

There has been a good deal of speculation as to the personal appearance of these foreigners and much has been made of the possibility that this life might be of such exotic aspect that we here at home would be unable to recognize it. An interesting thought indeed, but, alas, like all interesting thoughts it has at its core the basest sort of longing. For as an earthling who has seen, if not it all, then at least all that I care to, I cannot help but be reminded of that immutable truth: if you go looking for trouble you're bound to find it.

Under the impression that life makes itself evident only in the physical mode, the general public—a perennially lackluster bunch—tends to dwell on such matters as arms, noses, and neck size, thereby envisioning a being that differs from the average Joe only in the most superficial detail. Scientists—a crowd that when it comes to style and dash makes the general public look like the Bloomsbury Set—seem to speak largely of microbes, gases, and liquid states.

This concern with the corporeal is really superfluous. There is, of course, life on Mars and we shall, of course, recognize it, if not by its form, then most certainly by its function, which it undoubtedly shares with our own local brand of life: the will to annoy.

In order to recognize *which is life* we must first deal with the somewhat broader question of *what is life.* Here we discover that others have preceded us and provided quite a range of answers. We consider each answer individually but we are invariably disappointed. A bowl of cherries? Too pat. A cabaret? Not in this neighborhood. Real? Hardly. Earnest? Please.

It is by this painstaking method of careful examination and eventual rejection that we reach a conclusion: life is something to do when you can't get to sleep. Therefore, that which we call civilization is merely the accumulated debris of a chilling number of bad nights.

There is no reason to believe that the Martians are any less nervous than we are (indeed they are very likely more so—their insomnia compounded by the problems of living so far uptown) and therefore they are undoubtedly a thoroughly unpleasant lot.

Let us assume for the purposes of this essay that the Martians are microbes. Microbes are undeniably on the small side, which means that basketball and fashion models are definitely not in the picture. Such deficiency in size is worthy of comment, for the concept of an entire planet that cannot reach the top shelf is seriously disconcerting. Perhaps we can best understand these beings by a careful study of Mars as a whole.

Mars

It is generally accepted that Mars was named for the Roman god of war. This is erroneous. The closely guarded truth is that it was actually discovered by a Roman gentleman of artistic temperament who attempted to use his achievement to romantic advantage. The Roman, his eye on an attractive but elusive Swedish fellow, tried flattery. Great political pressure was brought to bear and he eventually came to understand that the Roman Empire had no intention of allowing any planet of theirs to be called Lars. As you can see, a compromise was reached.

The Land and Its Resources

Mars is the third smallest planet and therefore of interest only to collectors. It is bleak and rocky with no coastline to speak of—a feature that has made it one of the few beach areas within the financial grasp of this writer. Finding a taxi is next to impossible and visitors are advised not to.

Natural resources run heavily to alien vapors and strange stones.

The People and Their Work

The people, as has been stated before, are microbes—a condition that makes them at best peoplettes and at worst microbes. Their work consists mainly of getting visitors to stop making jokes about their height.

Population

This is difficult to determine unless one is prepared to look at the situation very closely.

Transportation

The favored mode of transportation is infecting a visitor and then hoping that he goes someplace.

Chief Products

The chief products of Mars are tiny little polyester leisure suits and miniature graduate schools.

City Limiting:
The New Geography

I had barely recovered from the appellative blow struck by SoHo (*So*uth of *Ho*uston Street) when I received a quick left to the sensibility in the form of NoHo (*No*rth of *Ho*uston Street). Head bloody but unbowed, I dropped my guard and TriBeCa (*Tri*angle *Be*low *Ca*nal Street) scored a T.K.O. in the very first sound.

I have been laid up now for quite a while and have had ample time to consider this matter in detail. Yes indeed, I've given this thing a lot of thought and I've come to the conclusion that this crazed naming of extremely specific areas of the city has yet to come to full flower. An appalling situation—no end in sight—there is not the slightest indication that these area buffs have named their last. It is abundantly clear that such vague terms as Midtown will no longer suffice; it will only get worse and will probably go something like this:

NoTifSoSher

NoTifSoSher (*No*rth of *Tif*fany's, *So*uth of the *Sher*ry-Netherland) is a two-block stretch of Fifth Avenue much favored by shoppers, hotel guests, and strollers from all walks of life. Its attractive jewelry displays and one-way traffic have made it one of the most desirable locations in the city. The undisputed king of the parade route, NoTifSoSher is beloved by Irishmen and war veterans alike. A must-see for taxi-hailers.

BeJelfth

A little-known section of town, BeJelfth is a whimsically placed block of West Fourth Street (*Be*tween *Ja*ne and Tw*elfth*). Truly a cabby stumper, BeJelfth is a favorite meeting place for dogs both large and small. The delicatessen on the corner is a veritable Mecca for thrill-seekers who never fail to be amazed by the dizzyingly skyrocketing prices.

Little Humility

Long a bastion of male camaraderie, this eccentrically shaped area is bounded on the east by the beginning of Christopher Street and on the west by the Hudson River. Although positively reeking with unconventional charm, Little Humility is a snap to find as it deviates not an inch from the beaten path and abounds with cunning little bars and irresistible tractor-trailer trucks. Those who frequent this district have every right (and every left) to refer to it proudly as the Keys to the City.

Food for Thought
and Vice Versa

Summer has an unfortunate effect upon hostesses who have been unduly influenced by the photography of Irving Penn and take the season as a cue to serve dinners of astonishingly meager proportions. These they call light, a quality which while most assuredly welcome in comedies, cotton shirts, and hearts, is not an appropriate touch at dinner.

It is not surprising that a number of such hostesses seem to be associated with the world of high fashion, for it follows that a person whose idea of a hard day's work is posing for Deborah Turbeville might also be of the opinion that parsley is an adequate meat course.

Thin, almost transparent slices of lemon do indeed go a long way in dressing up a meal but they should not be counted as a separate vegetable.

* * *

Cold soup is a very tricky thing and it is the rare hostess who can carry it off. More often than not the dinner guest is left with the impression that had he only come a little earlier he could have gotten it while it was still hot.

* * *

A salad is not a meal. It is a style.

* * *

Japanese food is very pretty and undoubtedly a suitable cuisine in Japan, which is largely populated by people of below average size. Hostesses hell-bent on serving such food to occidentals would be well advised to supplement it with something more substantial and to keep in mind that almost everybody likes french fries.

* * *

Vegetables are interesting but lack a senes of purpose when unaccompanied by a good cut of meat.

* * *

Water chestnuts are supposed to go in a thing, not to be the thing itself.

* * *

White grapes are very attractive but when it comes to dessert people generally like cake with icing.

* * *

Candied violets are the Necco Wafers of the overbred.

There are a number of restaurants in New York that cater primarily to the confirmed bachelor. These establishments share many characteristics with the summer hostess and then some.

One such local eatery is a remodeled diner that looks like what Busby Berkeley would have done if only he hadn't had the money. It is open twenty-four hours a day —one supposes as a convenience to the hungry truck driver who will belly up to the takeout counter and bellow, "Two cucumber soups—good and cold; one endive salad—red wine vinaigrette; and one order of fresh asparagus—hold the hollandaise."

Saffron should be used sparingly if at all. No matter how enamored one might be of this seasoning, there are few who would agree that it is equal to salt in the versatility department.

* * *

A native-born American who has spent the entire day in what he knows to be New York City and has not once stepped aboard a ship or plane is almost invariably chagrined and disoriented by a menu that uses the French counterpart for the perfectly adequate English word *grapefruit.*

* * *

Watercress is pleasant enough in a salad or sandwich, but when placed alongside a hamburger it is merely an annoyance.

* * *

While it is undeniably true that people love a surprise, it is equally true that they are seldom pleased to suddenly and without warning happen upon a series of prunes in what they took to be a normal loin of pork.

* * *

People have been cooking and eating for thousands of years, so if you are the very first to have thought of adding fresh lime juice to scalloped potatoes try to understand that there must be a reason for this.

Technological innovation has done great damage not only to reading habits but also to eating habits. Food is now available in such unpleasant forms that one frequently finds smoking between courses to be an aid to the digestion.

A loaf of bread that is more comfortable than a sofa cannot help but be unpalatable.

* * *

The servant problem being what it is, one would think it apparent that a society that provides a Helper for tuna but compels a writer to pack her own suitcases desperately needs to reorder its priorities.

* * *

Chocolate is an excellent flavor for ice cream but both unreasonable and disconcerting in chewing gum.

* * *

Breakfast cereals that come in the same colors as polyester leisure suits make oversleeping a virtue.

* * *

When one asks for cream one should receive either cream or the information that the establishment in question favors instead a combination of vegetable oil and cancer-causing initials.

* * *

Cheese that is required by law to append the word *food* to its title does not go well with red wine or fruit.

Thoroughly distasteful as synthetic foods might be, one cannot help but accord them a certain value when confronted with the health food buff. One is also ever mindful of the fact that the aficionado of whole foods is a frequent champion of excessive political causes.

* * *

Brown rice is ponderous, overly chewy, and possessed of unpleasant religious overtones.

* * *

Civilized adults do not take apple juice with dinner.

* * *

Inhabitants of underdeveloped nations and victims of natural disasters are the only people who have ever been happy to see soybeans.

* * *

Bread that must be sliced with an ax is bread that is too nourishing.

* * *

Large, naked, raw carrots are acceptable as food only to those who live in hutches eagerly awaiting Easter.

Food is such a common occurrence in our daily lives that few have taken the time to consider it in the broader sense and thus cannot truly appreciate its impact on society.

Food is welcome at both meal and snack time. It goes well with most any beverage and by and large makes the best sandwich.

* * *

Food gives real meaning to dining room furniture.

* * *

Food goes a long way in rounding out a CARE package.

* * *

Food offers the perfect excuse to use the good dishes.

* * *

Food is an important part of a balanced diet.

* * *

Food plays a crucial role in international politics. If there was no such thing as food, state dinners would be replaced by state bridge games and, instead of fasting, political activists would probably just whine.

* * *

A foodless world would have the disastrous effect of robbing one's initiative. Ambition has no place in a society that refuses its members the opportunity to become top banana.

* * *

Without food, one of man's most perplexing yet engaging problems would be rendered meaningless when one realized that the chicken and the egg both didn't come first.

* * *

If food did not exist it would be well-nigh impossible to get certain types off the phone, as one would be unable to say, "Look, I've got to run but let's have dinner sometime soon."

* * *

Food was a very big factor in Christianity. What would the miracle of the loaves and fishes have been without it? And the Last Supper—how effective would that have been?

* * *

If there was no such thing as food, Oyster Bay would be called just Bay, and for the title of *The Cherry Orchard* Chekhov would have chosen *A Group of Empty Trees, Regularly Spaced.*

Arts

Arts

Perhaps the least cheering statement ever made on the subject of art is that life imitates it. This would doubtless be more heartening news were its veracity not quite so capricious. For upon inspection it is immediately apparent that life is at its most artistic when such a condition is least desired. It is, in fact, safe to assume that, more often than not, life imitates craft, for who among us can say that our experience does not more closely resemble a macramé plant holder than it does a painting by Seurat. When it comes to art, life is the biggest copycat in the matter of the frame.

Wishing to investigate the matter more thoroughly, I gathered about me a group of like-minded associates and began the long, hard work of imitating art in its most contemporary manifestations.

Conceptual Art

We positioned ourselves randomly on a hardwood floor and pretended to be cinder blocks. We affixed to our shirtfronts labels bearing words unrelated to one another in a linear sense. We were not understood and we were greatly admired. We found this to be not un-fulfilling.

Graphic Design

Some of us dressed up like bold, daring lines; others, like large, clear, easy-to-read letters and numbers. All of us wore simple yet childish bright colors. We arranged ourselves in the shape of an airport and adopted a manner both useful and sprightly. We were most popular with those similarly dressed.

Magazine Layout

Quite a few of us wore the same things we had worn when following the example of Graphic Design, although we went to considerably smaller sizes. The rest of us divided ourselves equally into two groups—one being airbrushed color illustration; the other being out-of-context, blown-up quotations from articles. All of us stationed ourselves for maximum intrusion value. Everyone crowded together in the form of a single page but kept our distance by the clever use of numerous black borders. We were a big hit and proved once and for all that you can take the art out of art direction but you can't take the direction out of art, at least not if it's headed that way.

Furniture Design

We researched this one carefully and decided to be both fun and functional. We wore molded plastic, durable fabrics, and lots of butcher's block. We assumed the shapes of gigantic bean bags, inflatable rafts, hard-edged paintings, and cumulus clouds. We were rather reminded of our days as Graphic Design and felt more than ever that we had a multi-purpose in life.

Architecture

We thought a lot about glass and new, lightweight building materials. We imagined ourselves schools, shopping centers, office buildings, public housing, and luxury apartment complexes. We hoped that at least a few of the others would imagine themselves signs so that people could tell us apart.

Popular Music

We attired ourselves in shiny garments so as to accurately reflect the hopes and dreams of the general public. We entered elevators, cars, planes, telephones, and just about every place else you couldn't think of. We were an inescapable influence on the culture and inspired a fanatical devotion, for we made a joyful noise unto the bored.

Movies

We were careful to adopt only those attitudes associated with work of serious intention, being well aware that life generally does not imitate entertainment. We exhibited extreme sensitivity and technical prowess while motioning lyrically. We explored the themes of violence, despair, and social injustice that lurk beneath the slick surface of our society. We were nice and quiet, saying little and keeping pretty much to ourselves.

Fashion

Some of us borrowed quite heavily from others. Some of us were unduly imaginative. A lot of us felt silly making these statements but we attempted to invest them with deeper meaning. This was not, in light of the preponderance of polyester, easy, but people bought it. Believing us to be expressions of their true personalities, the public clasped us to their bosoms and added a few fun touches of their own.

Not in the:
Mood Jewelry

As one whose taste in mental states has always run largely toward the coma, I have very little patience with the current craze for self-awareness. I am already far too well acquainted with how I feel and frankly, given the choice, I would not. Anyone who is troubled by the inability to feel his or her own feelings is more than welcome to feel mine. It should not be surprising, then, for you to learn that I am something less than enchanted with a concept such as mood jewelry. For those of you fortunate enough to have your lack of awareness extend into the realm of advertising, mood jewelry is jewelry that tells you your feelings via a heat-sensitive stone. And although one would think that stones would have quite enough to do, what with graves and walls and such, it seems that they have now taken on the job of informing people that they are nervous. And although one would think that a person who is nervous would be more than able to ascertain that fact without the aid of a quite unattractive ring, this is apparently not the case.

Mood jewelry comes to us in many guises: necklaces,

rings, watches, and bracelets. But whatever form it takes, it is invariably equipped with the perceptive and informative stone that not only relates one's present mood but also indicates in what direction that mood is headed. The stone performs this newsy feat by means of color change. The following, chosen solely on the basis of crankiness, has been excerpted from an ad:

EACH COLOR CHANGE
REVEALS THE INNER YOU!

ONYX BLACK . . . Overworked.

AMBER RED . . . You are becoming more strained, even anxious.

TOPAZ YELLOW . . . Somewhat unsettled, your mind is wandering.

JADE GREEN . . . Normal, nothing unusual is happening.

TURQUOISE BLUE-GREEN . . . You are beginning to relax . . . your emotions are turning up.

LAPIS BLUE . . . You feel comfortable . . . you belong. Relax . . . your feelings are beginning to flow freely.

SAPPHIRE BLUE . . . You're completely open . . . feeling happy . . . concentrating on your strong inner feelings and passions. This is the highest state.

One can safely assume that a person who finds it necessary to consult a bracelet on the subject of his own state of mind is a person who is undoubtedly perplexed by a great many things. It follows, then, that in such a case a piece of jewelry that reveals only emotions can hardly be called adequate—for here is a person besieged and beset by questions far more complex than "Am I strained?" This is an individual who needs *answers*—an individual who should be able to look at his heavily adorned wrist and ask, "Am I tall? Short? A natural blond? A man? A woman? An elm? Do I own my own home? Can I take a joke? Do I envy the success of others?"

Clearly, if there is to be such a thing as mood jewelry it must become more specific. In the interests of hastening such an occurrence I offer the following:

THE FRAN LEBOWITZ GUIDE
TO EVEN GREATER SELF-TRUTHS THROUGH COLOR CHANGE!

REDDISH BEIGE . . . You are an American Indian who is boring . . . you are of little interest both to yourself and to other American Indians.

BEIGISH RED . . . You are a white person who is boring . . . you are deeply embarrassed by your complete lack of interesting qualities . . . humility is no substitute for a good personality . . . this will not change.

LAVENDER . . . You are either a homosexual or a bathroom rug in a house where you match the tile . . . if you decide in favor of being a bathroom rug just remember that as a homosexual you could have been on the David Susskind Show.

HORIZONTAL STRIPES . . . You are extremely thin and have reacted to this fact excessively . . . this is the lowest state.

MULATTO . . . One of your parents is turning into a Negro . . . if your parents are already Negroes one of them is turning into a white person.

IRREGULAR, FINE LINES . . . You are getting somewhat older . . . this will probably continue.

BURNT UMBER . . . You are turning into an artist . . . possibly Hans Holbein, the Younger. This is the highest state.

Clothes with Pictures and/or Writing on Them: Yes—Another Complaint

Now, I'm not just talking about Vuitton bags. Or Gucci wallets. Or Hermès scarves. Designers and/or business concerns who splash their names and initials all over overpriced accoutrements of dubious quality are of course sorely lacking in taste, but I am not going to be sidetracked by trivialities. I'm talking about the larger issues. Open-necked Deco-ish shirts with a repeating pattern of middle-sized silhouettes of sailboats. Blue jeans depicting the death of Marilyn Monroe in waterproof pastels. Dresses upon which one (but preferably two) can play Monopoly. Overalls that remind toddlers, through the use of small pink animals spouting comic strip balloons, to brush their teeth. T-shirts that proclaim the illegal sexual preferences of the wearer. Etcetera. Etcetera.

While clothes with pictures and/or writing on them are not entirely an invention of the modern age, they are an unpleasant indication of the general state of things. The particular general state of things that I am referring to is the general state of things that encourages people to express themselves through their clothing.

Frankly, I for one would not be unhappy if most people expressed themselves by marching en masse into the nearest large body of water but, barring that, I wish they would at least stop attempting to tell all by word of jacket. I mean, be realistic. If people don't want to listen to *you,* what makes you think they want to hear from your sweater?

There are two main reasons why we wear clothes. First, to hide figure flaws, of which the average person has at least seventeen. And second, to look cute, which is at least cheering. If some people think that nice, muted solid colors are a bit dull they can add some punch with stripes, plaids, checks, or—if it's summer and they're girls—small dots. And for those of you who feel that this is too restrictive, answer me this: If God meant for people to walk around in coats that have pictures of butterscotch sundaes on them, then why does *he* wear Tattersall shirts?

Soho:
Or Not at Home with Mr. Art

Soho is a real place. By real I mean that it exists materially. Mr. Art is not a real person. By not a real person I mean that he does not exist materially. Nevertheless, where Soho is concerned I wouldn't consider excluding Mr. Art from my observations, for in matters such as this he is my most trusted adviser and confidant. He is a dapper little fellow, perhaps a bit wry—and while it has been said of him that his manner cannot really support his mannerisms, he is, I can assure you, a welcome relief from some of these other types we get in here.

I will introduce you to Soho slowly by noting that this area of downtown Manhattan shares with Mr. Art nary a single characteristic. Up until a few years ago Soho was an obscure district of lofts used chiefly for storage and light manufacturing. It wasn't called Soho then—it wasn't called anything because no one ever went there except the people who make Christmas tree ornaments out of styrofoam and glitter or fabric trimmings out of highly colored stretch felt. And say what you will about members of these professions, they are generally, I am sure, very nice people who not only don't make those things out of choice but also don't go around calling obscure districts of Manhattan things like Soho. Ostensibly, Soho is called Soho because it begins *So*uth of *Ho*uston Street, but if you want my opinion I wouldn't be too terribly surprised to discover that the person who thought up this name is a person whose circle of friends in 1967 included at least one too many English photographer. It was, of course, a combination of many unattractive things that led to the Soho of today, but quite definitely the paramount factor was the advent of Big Art. Before Big Art came along, painters lived, as God undoubtedly intended them to, in garrets or remodeled carriage houses, and painted paintings of a reasonable size. A painting of a reasonable size is a painting that one can easily hang over a sofa. If a painting cannot be easily hung over a sofa it is obviously a painting painted by a painter who got too big for his brushes and is in fact the very sort of painting responsible for Mr. Art's chronically curled upper lip. Painters, however, are not the only ones involved here. Modern sculptors, or *those chiselers* as Mr. Art is wont to call them, must bear a good part of the blame, for when clay and marble went out and demolished tractor-trailer trucks came in, Big Art was here to stay.

One day a Big Artist realized that if he took all of the sewing machines and bales of rags out of a three-thousand-square-foot loft and put in a bathroom and kitchen he would be able to live and make Big Art in the same place. He was quickly followed by other Big Artists and they by Big Lawyers, Big Boutique Owners, and Big Rich Kids. Soon there was a Soho and it was positively awash in hardwood floors, talked-to plants, indoor swings, enormous record collections, hiking boots, Conceptual Artists, video communes, Art book stores, Art grocery stores, Art restaurants, Art bars, Art galleries, and boutiques selling tie-dyed raincoats, macramé flower pots, and Art Deco salad plates.

Since the beginning of the Soho of today the only people in New York who have been able to get through a
Saturday afternoon without someone calling them on
the telephone to suggest that they go down to Soho and
look at the Art are those who belong to Black Nationalist
organizations. As neither myself nor Mr. Art is a member of such a group, we consider it quite a feather in our
mutual cap that we have succumbed to these ofttimes
strongly worded suggestions so infrequently, and that
on the rare occasions that we have we certainly have not
been gracious about it.

A recent Saturday was just such an occasion and here
is what we saw:

Art Gallery Number One

A girl who would probably have been a welcome addition to the teaching staff of any progressive nursery
school in the country had instead taken it upon herself
to create out of ceramic clay exact replicas of such
leather objects as shoes, boots, suitcases, and belts.
There was no question but that she had achieved her
goal—one had literally to snap one's fingernail against
each object and hear it ring before one was convinced
that what one was snapping one's fingernail against
was indeed ceramic clay and not leather. And one could,
of course, choose to ignore Mr. Art as he hissed, "Why
bother?" and struck a match across a pair of gloves in
order to light one of his aromatic foreign cigarettes.

Art Gallery Number Two

A young man who had apparently been refused admission to the Boy Scouts on moral grounds had arranged on a shiny oak floor several groups of rocks. He
had then murdered a number of adolescent birch trees
in order to bend them into vaguely circular shapes and

hang them on the wall. These things were all for sale at prices that climbed well into the thousands. "First of all, imagine actually wanting to *own* any of this stuff," sneered Mr. Art, "and then imagine not being able to figure out that with an ax and a wheelbarrow you could make it all yourself in a single morning and still have time to talk to your plants."

Art Gallery Number Three

Two boys who were really good friends had taken a trip to North Africa. They took a lot of color photographs of bowls, skies, pipes, animals, water, and each other. They had arranged the photographs alphabetically—i.e., A—Ashes, B—Bright sunny day—pasted them to pieces of varnished plywood, written intricately simple little explanations beneath each photograph, and hung them under their appropriate letters. I am compelled to admit that upon viewing this work Mr. Art had to be forcibly restrained from doing bodily harm to himself and those around him.

Art Gallery Number Four

Someone who had spent a deservedly lonely childhood in movie theaters had gotten hold of a lot of stills from forties films, cut out the faces of the stars, handcolored them, and pasted them to blow-ups of picture postcards from Hollywood and Las Vegas. "Too camp," said Mr. Art testily upon being awakened; "they oughta lock 'em all up."

Art Galleries Number Five Through Sixteen

Scores of nine-by-twelve photo-realist renderings of gas stations, refrigerators, pieces of cherry pie, art col-

lectors, diners, '59 Chevys, and Mediterranean-style dining room sets.

Mr. Art and I are presently seeking membership in a
Black Nationalist organization. In the meantime we
have taken our phone off the hook.

Color:
Drawing the Line

Color is, of course, not wholly without virtue. Shape being insufficient, it is necessary that things possess a certain measure of color in order that they might be distinguished one from the other. It would hardly do if in reaching for a cigarette one picked up a pen and discovered that the prospect of a moment's relaxation had turned instead into hours of tedious labor. It is, however, doubtful in the extreme that the degree of color demanded by simple distinction bears any relation whatsoever to such a concept as lime green.

I am not, I assure you, totally unreceptive to color providing it makes its appearance quietly, deferentially, and without undue fanfare. I am compelled to make this statement in view of the current popular belief that color is capable of conveying ideas and supplying us with a key to the human personality. This type of thing has become far too prevalent and I for one absolutely and unequivocally refuse to be bullied about by a thing's capacity to absorb light. There is nothing less appealing than a color fraught with meaning—the very notion is boisterous, inappropriate, and marked by the dreariest sort of longing.

Due to the urgent nature of this situation it is necessary that purely aesthetic considerations be allied with the equally grave concerns of philosophical error. The entire matter has too long been ignored—a hue and cry are long overdue.

The Primary Colors

The primary colors are the most blatantly abused. Chief offenders can be divided into two main camps.

First, the graphic design crowd who think that primary colors are both cheering and bold and demonstrate this belief by employing them incessantly in places where people have every right to be depressed. In fact, so widespread is the use of red, yellow, and blue in schools, airports, and cancer hospitals that, should one find oneself with neither textbook nor luggage in a place thus adorned, one could not be accused of overreacting were one to decide to jump.

Second, there are those who endeavor too stridently to impart an aura of passion, childlike innocence, or serenity, depending upon which primary color they have chosen. The concern here is, of course, not with those who use these colors moderately but rather with those who, lacking the personality to get carried away with themselves, are forced instead to get carried away with someone else.

Red

Red is frequently associated with passion because it is the color of fire. Those who take this seriously need to be reminded that there is such a thing as arson.

Yellow

People who favor yellow with inordinate gusto are attempting to create an air of childlike innocence and sunny optimism. As these particular properties cannot possibly be the reason for the color of warning signals and legal pads, one would be well advised to look both ways before crossing.

Blue

Blue is supposed to indicate serenity because it is the supposed color of water, which is supposedly a calm and restful element. In dealing with champions of this hue one could do worse than remember that water is also the favorite environment of sharks and the cause, nine times out of nine, of death by drowning.

The Secondary Colors

The secondary colors—green, orange, and purple—are merely variations on a theme. They, like the primary colors, have their place and are often, I am told, found in nature.

Despite all this I remain, where color is concerned, less than enthusiastic. There are those who contend that without it the world would be a very dull place indeed—and then again there are those who contend that at least it wouldn't clash.

The Sound of Music:
Enough Already

First off, I want to say that as far as I am concerned, in instances where I have not personally and deliberately sought it out, the only difference between music and Muzak is the spelling. Pablo Casals practicing across the hall with the door open—being trapped in an elevator, the ceiling of which is broadcasting "Parsley, Sage, Rosemary, and Thyme"—it's all the same to me. Harsh words? Perhaps. But then again these are not gentle times we live in. And they are being made no more gentle by this incessant melody that was once real life.

There was a time when music knew its place. No longer. Possibly this is not music's fault. It may be that music fell in with a bad crowd and lost its sense of common decency. I am willing to consider this. I am willing even to try and help. I would like to do my bit to set music straight in order that it might shape up and leave the mainstream of society. The first thing that music must understand is that there are two kinds of music—good music and bad music. Good music is music that I want to hear. Bad music is music that I don't want to hear.

So that music might more clearly see the error of its ways I offer the following. If you are music and you recognize yourself on this list, you are bad music.

1. Music in Other People's Clock Radios

There are times when I find myself spending the night in the home of another. Frequently the other is in a more reasonable line of work than I and must arise at a specific hour. Ofttimes the other, unbeknownst to me, manipulates an appliance in such a way that I am awakened by Stevie Wonder. On such occasions I announce that if I wished to be awakened by Stevie Wonder I would sleep with Stevie Wonder. I do not, however, wish to be awakened by Stevie Wonder and that is why God invented alarm clocks. Sometimes the other realizes that I am right. Sometimes the other does not. And that is why God invented *many* others.

2. Music Residing in the Hold Buttons of Other People's Business Telephones

I do not under any circumstances enjoy hold buttons. But I am a woman of reason. I can accept reality. I can face the facts. What I cannot face is the music. Just as there are two kinds of music—good and bad—so there are two kinds of hold buttons—good and bad. Good hold buttons are hold buttons that hold one silently. Bad hold buttons are hold buttons that hold one musically. When I hold I want to hold silently. That is the way it was meant to be, for that is what God was talking about when he said, "Forever hold your peace." He would have added, "and quiet," but he thought you were smarter.

3. Music in the Streets

The past few years have seen a steady increase in the number of people playing music in the streets. The past few years have also seen a steady increase in the number of malignant diseases. Are these two facts related? One wonders. But even if they are not—and, as I have pointed out, one cannot be sure—music in the streets has definitely taken its toll. For it is at the very least disorienting. When one is walking down Fifth Avenue, one does not expect to hear a string quartet playing a Strauss waltz. What one expects to hear while walking down Fifth Avenue is traffic. When one does indeed hear a string quartet playing a Strauss waltz while one is walking down Fifth Avenue, one is apt to become confused and imagine that one is not walking down Fifth Avenue at all but rather that one has somehow wound up in Old Vienna. Should one imagine that one is in Old Vienna one is likely to become quite upset when one realizes that in Old Vienna there is no sale at Charles Jourdan. And that is why when I walk down Fifth Avenue I want to hear traffic.

4. Music in the Movies

I'm not talking about musicals. Musicals are movies that warn you by saying, "Lots of music here. Take it or leave it." I'm talking about regular movies that extend no such courtesy but allow unsuspecting people to come to see them and then assault them with a barrage of unasked-for tunes. There are two major offenders in this category: black movies and movies set in the fifties. Both types of movies are afflicted with the same misconception. They don't know that movies are supposed to be movies. They think that movies are supposed to be records with pictures. They have failed to understand that if God had wanted records to have pictures, he would not have invented television.

5. *Music in Public Places Such as Restaurants, Supermarkets, Hotel Lobbies, Airports, Etc.*

When I am in any of the above-mentioned places I am not there to hear music. I am there for whatever reason is appropriate to the respective place. I am no more interested in hearing "Mack the Knife" while waiting for the shuttle to Boston than someone sitting ringside at the Sands Hotel is interested in being forced to choose between sixteen varieties of cottage cheese. If God had meant for everything to happen at once, he would not have invented desk calendars.

Epilogue

Some people talk to themselves. Some people sing to themselves. Is one group better than the other? Did not God create all people equal? Yes, God created all people equal. Only to some he gave the ability to make up their own words.

A Brush with Death

Perhaps one of the more noteworthy trends of our time is the occupation of buildings accompanied by the taking of hostages. The perpetrators of these deeds are generally motivated by political grievance, social injustice, and the deeply felt desire to see how they look on TV. They are a bold lot—reckless and driven—true champions of equal time.

Although repeatedly in the news, these events were more often than not ignored in artistic circles. This element was unconcerned and felt far removed from such occurrences, lacking as they were in visual impact. Their complacency was, however, rudely shattered by a series of incidents that stunned the art world with their daring use of local color and imposing command of space.

Incident No. 1—"Untitled" (Gasoline on Rag)

A small band of exiled Cubists took over the Great Rotunda in the Capitol Building in Washington, D.C., and threatened to set it on fire unless the entire city was broken down into its basic geometric forms. They took as hostages Three Musicians and announced to the media that unless their demands were met the violinist would be forced at gunpoint to, in the words of Braque X, the leader of the group, "fiddle while domes burned."

Desperate to avoid such a tragedy, government officials conferred through the night, and on the following morning an Abstract Expressionist was sent in to negotiate a peaceful settlement. The Abstract Expressionist, a crafty fellow with a long history of pulling the wool over people's eyes, seemed to be making some headway until Braque X accused him of having no perspective on the subject. This delayed the proceedings for hours but eventually the Abstract Expressionist, who had every reason to want the Cubists out of the picture, calmed Braque X by guaranteeing safe passage if he promised to give up his crazy scheme. Braque X, realizing that they had him up against the wall, accepted the offer and an assemblage of planes and angles transported the Cubists back to their rightful place in art history.

The police, however, were not satisfied with the outcome and the commanding officer, with a hard edge to his voice, declared in an interview, "My five-year-old daughter could do better than that." This opinion captured the imagination of the public and a vigilante committee was quickly formed. Late that night the Abstract Expressionist was escorted by a firing squad out into the middle of a color field and splattered with bullets—another victim of shifting tastes.

Incident No. 2—"Girl with Submachine Gun"

A group of feminist artists known as Women Against took hostage a group of male representational painters and demanded to know why they depicted women as

having breasts. The men answered that they painted
women with breasts because women had breasts, and
accused the feminists of fear of framing. The women
instantly saw the wisdom of this and apologized profusely, explaining that they were severely depressed because they were all having their Blue Period.

Incident No. 3—"Form Following a Function"

The good eye of the whole world was upon a small
Italian town when a revolutionary terrorist organization known as the Bauhaus Bombers threatened to turn
the Leaning Tower of Pisa into a machine for dying by
blowing it up. Intent on avoiding clutter, the Bauhaus
Bombers took no hostages but demanded instead that
one purely decorative object be destroyed every hour on
the hour until their goal was achieved. Just what this
goal was, was not known, for they insisted upon secrecy
unless proof could be shown that no other terrorist organization had designs on it. Fearing the loss of the historic building, officials acquiesced totally. Truckloads of
bric-a-brac were brought into the town square. Under
the direction of the Bombers, dozens and dozens of
china figurines, clever wall hangings, and superfluous
vases were sacrificed to the mysterious cause.

Time went on and still the terrorists refused to divulge their purpose. Daily the crowds grew more restive
and the police, faced with the possibility of a riot, finally
devised a plan of action. By dressing one of their number in rust-colored wide-wale corduroy and a black tur-
tleneck sweater, they managed to infiltrate the organization. In due time intelligence reached them that the
arsenal they had envisioned was instead one mere
bomb of exceedingly meager proportions. Astonished
that the Bombers would equip themselves so minimally,
they questioned their agent as to the reason for this

folly. Having spent a good deal of time in the tower he simply looked at them coolly and remarked, "Less is more."

Much relieved, the police entered the building and easily overcame their adversaries. Once in custody the Bauhaus Bombers spoke freely, maintaining passionately that their cause was just. All they wanted, they said, was for the Leaning Tower of Pisa to be straightened out. Asked why such extreme measures had been taken, they shouted, "Never again!" They then leveled their final and unarguable charge against the sinking edifice: that the Leaning Tower of Pisa was and continues to be blatantly anti-symmetric.

Incident No. 4—"Reclining Chair and Toaster Eating Licorice"

A small but incongruous group of the followers of Dada known as MOMA all dressed in pants and went to the outskirts of Chicago. They then sent a message to the President of the United States demanding a more amusing juxtaposition of laws. Before the President could respond, a well-known consumer advocate charged the members of MOMA with lining a teacup with the pelt of an endangered species. The Dadaists were brought before a Senate subcommittee and forced to accept the terms of an agreement that would compel them in the future to use fun fur or none at all. The members of MOMA bridled at this restriction, as synthetic fabrics had already taken their toll by rendering an iron with nails in it far less witty than was originally thought. Looking back in retrospect, the Senate strictures were a blessing in disguise, enabling the Dadaists to realize that they had invented a form that lent itself to museums—which thereby lifted their spirits and gave them all a good laugh.

Incident No. 5—"   "

A frightening number of conceptual artists (two) occupied space in downtown Manhattan and, when no one
noticed, were obliged to go uptown. There they arranged
some rocks in a pattern that announced that they were
holding hostage one hundred and sixty-eight videotape
cassettes. They demanded that people imagine that this
was of any interest. When no response was forthcoming
they congratulated themselves heartily on their success
and repeated the action endlessly.

Letters

Letters

Owing to the conditions that currently prevail in the world of letters, it is now possible for a girl to be ruined by a book. Owing, in fact, to the conditions that currently prevail in the world of letters, it is now possible for a boy to be ruined by a book.

A book, of course, is not the only danger, for things have come to such a pass that a magazine is safer than a book only to the extent that it is shorter. But magazines all too frequently lead to books and should be regarded by the prudent as the heavy petting of literature.

This warning should be heeded by all concerned, and in order to bring about a less perilous printed environment, I offer the following tips on how to avoid the reading and/or writing of ruinous material.

Women's Books

Enroll in medical school and specialize in gynecology. It will not be long before disenchantment sets in and you realize that the literary possibilities of the vulva have been somewhat overestimated.

* * *

Women who insist upon having the same options as men would do well to consider the option of being the strong, silent type.

* * *

Having been unpopular in high school is not just cause for book publication.

* * *

Having been popular in high school should have been enough. Do not share this experience with the reading public.

* * *

If your sexual fantasies were truly of interest to others, they would no longer be fantasies.

* * *

As an aficionado of literature it might interest you to know that, in all of Shakespeare, the word *assertive* appears not a single time.

* * *

Keep in mind that there are still certain subjects that are unsuitable at the table, and that a great many people read while eating.

Poetry

If you are of the opinion that the contemplation of suicide is sufficient evidence of a poetic nature, do not forget that actions speak louder than words.

* * *

Generally speaking, it is inhumane to detain a fleeting insight.

* * *

The free lunch was originated by saloonkeepers during the Depression. Free verse also often originates during depression. If this happens to you, try to nip it in the bud by taking a drink.

* * *

If, while watching the sun set on a used-car lot in Los Angeles, you are struck by the parallels between this image and the inevitable fate of humanity, do not, under any circumstances, write it down.

Special-Interest Magazines

Being a woman is of special interest only to aspiring male transsexuals. To actual women, it is simply a good excuse not to play football.

* * *

Special-interest publications should realize that if they are attracting enough advertising and readers to make a profit, the interest is not so special.

* * *

The exchange of information concerning the whereabouts of the best down comforter or chicken tandoori in New York should, I guess, be permitted between consenting adults in private so long as the young and the literate are left unmolested.

* * *

Sexual congress with heavy machinery is not a special interest. It is a personality defect.

Self-Help Books

There is no such word as *actualize*. There is no such word as *internalize*. There is, in fact, but one instance where the letters *ize* are appropriate here and that is in the word *fertilize*.

* * *

Mental health is rarely, if ever, achieved by reliving your birth in a bathtub.

* * *

If you want to get ahead in this world, get a lawyer—not a book.

* * *

Wealth and power are much more likely to be the result of breeding than they are of reading.

* * *

While it may occasionally occur that one's character shows in one's face, this is nothing to count on, for one's face will show in one's character long before that possibility has had a chance to arise.

Writing:
A Life Sentence

Contrary to what many of you might imagine, a career in letters is not without its drawbacks—chief among them the unpleasant fact that one is frequently called upon to actually sit down and write. This demand is peculiar to the profession and, as such, galling, for it is a constant reminder to the writer that he is not now, nor will he ever really be, like other men. For the requirements of the trade are so unattractive, so not fair, and so foreign to regular people that the writer is to the real world what Esperanto is to the language world—funny, maybe, but not *that* funny. This being the case, I feel the time has come for all concerned to accept the writer's differences as inherent and acknowledge once and for all that in the land of the blind the one-eyed man is a writer and he's not too thrilled about it.

Thus I offer the following with the hope that it will bring about much-needed compassion. Points 1 through 5 are for parents—the later explication for masochists. Or vice versa.

The Fran Lebowitz reader.

3800501264599

Sat May 28 2022

TANASE, COSTIN

How to Tell if Your Child Is a Writer

Your child is a writer if one or more of the following statements are applicable. Truthfulness is advised—no amount of fudging will alter the grim reality.

1. Prenatal

   A. You have morning sickness at night because the fetus finds it too distracting to work during the day.

   B. You develop a craving for answering services and typists.

   C. When your obstetrician applies his stethoscope to your abdomen he hears excuses.

2. Birth

   A. The baby is at least three weeks late because he had a lot of trouble with the ending.

   B. You are in labor for twenty-seven hours because the baby left everything until the last minute and spent an inordinate amount of time trying to grow his toes in a more interesting order.

   C. When the doctor spanks the baby the baby is not at all surprised.

   D. It is definitely a single birth because the baby has dismissed being twins as too obvious.

3. Infancy

   A. The baby refuses both breast and bottle, preferring instead Perrier with a twist in preparation for giving up drinking.

   B. The baby sleeps through the night almost immediately. Also through the day.

   C. The baby's first words, uttered at the age of four days, are "Next week."

   D. The baby uses teething as an excuse not to learn to gurgle.

   E. The baby sucks his forefinger out of a firm conviction that the thumb's been done to death.

4. Toddlerhood

A. He rejects teddy bears as derivative.

B. He arranges his alphabet blocks so as to spell out derisive puns on the names of others.

C. When he is lonely he does not ask his mother for a baby brother or sister but rather for a protégé.

D. When he reaches the age of three he considers himself a trilogy.

E. His mother is afraid to remove his crayoned handiwork from the living room walls lest she be accused of excessive editing.

F. When he is read his bedtime story he makes sarcastic remarks about style.

5. Childhood

A. At age seven he begins to think about changing his name. Also his sex.

B. He balks at going to summer camp because he is aware that there may be children there who have never heard of him.

C. He tells his teachers that he didn't do his homework because he was blocked.

D. He refuses to learn how to write a Friendly Letter because he knows he never will.

E. With an eye to a possible movie deal, he insists upon changing the title of his composition "What I Did on My Summer Vacation" to the far snappier "Vacation."

F. He is thoroughly hypochondriac and is convinced that his chicken pox is really leprosy.

G. On Halloween he goes out trick-or-treating dressed as Harold Acton.

By the time this unfortunate child has reached puberty there is no longer any hope that he will outgrow being a writer and become something more appealing —like a kidnap victim. The concern, then, as he enters the difficult period of adolescence, is that he receive the proper education in a sympathetic environment. For this reason it is strongly recommended that the teen writer attend a school geared to his dilemma—Writing High. At Writing High the student will be among his own kind—the ungrateful. He will be offered a broad range of subjects relevant to his needs: Beginning Badly, Avoiding Los Angeles One and Too, Remedial Wakefulness, Magazine Editors: Why?, and Advanced Deftness of Phrase—all taught by jealous teachers who would really rather be students. Extracurricular activities (such as the Jacket Flap Club, where students have fun while learning the rudiments of acquiring colorful temporary jobs such as lumberjack, numbers runner, shepherd, and pornographer) are in plentiful supply. The figure of speech team, the Metaphors, are mighty effective. They can mix it up with the best of them, and Janet Flanner, their lovable mascot, is a great campus favorite.

Although the yearbook—*The Contempt*—is rarely finished in time for graduation, it is nevertheless a treasured memento of the years spent at Writing High. The cafeteria is presided over by an overweight woman of great ambition and serves mediocre Italian food at ridiculously inflated prices. School spirit is encouraged by holding in the auditorium a weekly gathering known as Asimile. Tutoring is available for the slow student, or "ghost," as he is referred to at Writing High. Upon graduation or expulsion (and expulsion is favored by the more commercial students, who prize it for its terrific possibilities as a talk-show anecdote) the writer is as ready as he'll ever be to make his mark upon the world.

It is unnecessary to detail the next, or actual career, stage, for all writers end up the same—either dead or in Homes for the Aged Writer. The prospect of being put in such an establishment is viewed by all writers with great dread and not without reason. Recent scandals have revealed the shockingly widespread sadistic practice of slipping the aged writer unfavorable reviews, and more than one such victim has been found dead from lack of sufficient praise.

Not a very pretty picture, I'm afraid, and not a very accurate one either. But don't be encouraged by *that*—two wrongs don't make you write.

In Hot Pursuit

There recently appeared in the *New York Post* an article concerning the sexual abuse and exploitation of several thousand young boys in the Los Angeles area. Hard facts were on the sparse side but the police department did make some estimates:

> More than 3,000 children under the age of fourteen are being exploited sexually in the Los Angeles area.

> At least 2,000 local adult males actively pursue boys under the age of fourteen.

> More than 25,000 juveniles from fourteen to seventeen years of age are used sexually by approximately 15,000 adult males.

I was, of course, surprised to see so many numbers on a list of what were admittedly allegations and wondered just where they had gotten their figures. It was difficult to imagine the police actually going around counting, so instead I imagined this:

A Study in Harlots

In thinking back on the many exhilarating and arduous adventures that I have shared with my friend Mr. Sherlock Homes and Gardens, I can recall none more perplexing (or more fun) than that which I have chosen to call *A Study in Harlots.* Of course, *The Case of Dom Pérignon 1966* presented its problems, *The Afghan Hound of the Baskervilles* was hardly easy, and *The Baker Street Extremely Irregulars* was no piece of chicken, but none was a match for the tale I now tell.

First, allow me to introduce myself. I am Dr. John Watson, although Homes and Gardens often refers to me simply as "my dear." I am a qualified physician with a limited practice in the East Sixties (right near Halston's) and, I must say, much in demand, for between my own work and my association with Homes and Gardens it is generally acknowledged that Dr. John Watson knows exactly where all the bodies are buried. Homes and Gardens and I dwelt, of course, for many years at 221–B Baker Street, but the plummeting pound and outrageous taxes drove us from London, just as it did Mick, Liz, and so many other of our friends. We have taken up residence in Manhattan at an excellent address between Park and Madison (right near Halston's) and it is here that our story begins.

It was approximately eleven o'clock on a pleasant morning in early December when I descended the staircase of our tastefully appointed duplex penthouse. Homes and Gardens, an earlier riser than I, had already breakfasted and was lying, eyes closed, on the damask-covered Empire Récamier. Edward, a very attractive young man whose acquaintance we had recently made, played Homes and Gardens's violin for him. Homes and Gardens used, of course, to play his own violin, but that was before we made it. Homes and Gardens stretched a languid hand in greeting, his well-cut silk Saint Lau-

rent shirtsleeve in graceful folds around his wrist, and
said, "Watson, my dear, I see that you are a bit weary
after your long evening in which you first attended a
cocktail party in honor of Bill Blass's new sheet collection, had dinner at Pearl's with a number of fashion
notables, drank brandy at Elaine's with a well-known
author, danced at Regine's with a famous person's
daughter, and then went downtown to do it with a stran-
ger." I fell into a Louis XVI Marquise and looked at
Homes and Gardens wonderingly, for all my years of
being roommates with him had done nothing to dimin-
ish my astonishment at his remarkable powers of de-
duction. "How did you know?" I asked as soon as I had
regained my composure. "I didn't see you at all yesterday, for you were busy being photographed for *L'Uomo
Vogue* and I had no chance to tell you of my plans."
"Elementary, my dear: The first four items I observed
this morning in *Women's Wear Daily,* the last I deduced
by noting that your indigo blue Jackie Rogers jacket is
lying more smoothly than usual against your seriously
white Viyella sweater, indicating that your somewhat
recherché Fendi wallet is missing." My hand flew to my
inside breast pocket but I knew it was futile, for Homes
and Gardens was never wrong. "There, there, Watson
my dear, no use getting into a snit about it—your wallet
for a moment's pleasure is a rough trade, to be sure, but
I think I have something that will take your mind off
your loss. This morning there was a message on the
service from Precious Little asking that we take the
next flight to Los Angeles, as my assistance is required
in a matter of no small delicacy."

Precious Little was an interesting fellow, though
rather given to ancestor worship (other people's ances-
tors—he had none of his own to speak of) and Homes
and Gardens had known him for years. His association
with the Los Angeles Police Department was not exactly
professional. He was not an officer of the law or even

really a crime buff—it was, to be perfectly frank, quite simply that he had a most singular fondness for uniforms. Whatever his shortcomings, Precious was on the right side of the law and Homes and Gardens had aided him previously.

"Have our bags packed, my dear," said Homes and Gardens as he reached for the cocaine bottle, "I'll just do a few lines and then we must depart immediately." I made all haste and soon found myself sitting comfortably in the first-class compartment of a 747. A young woman in an ill-fitting pantsuit came to take our drink order. Homes and Gardens looked at her keenly yet disdainfully and said, "Stolichnaya straight up—for I can see that you had a difficult time of it, what with the five whiskey sours you consumed before finally meeting that account executive, and the poor-quality but large quantity of marijuana that you smoked with the sales manager you ran into this morning when leaving the account executive's apartment in the East Seventies near Third Avenue." The young woman gasped in disbelief and stuttered, "But, sir—how did you—how did you . . . ?"

"Elementary," he said coolly, "all stewardesses are alike."

I chuckled appreciatively. Homes and Gardens turned to me and said, "Now, my dear, I will tell you all that Precious told me, so that you are prepared to observe me observing the situation. It seems that a certain captain in the Los Angeles Police Department, you know who I mean, has been giving estimates to the press about the number of people involved in an underage homosexual sex scandal. Precious feels (and not without reason) that the situation is being exaggerated—you know how our captain brags—and I have been asked to investigate the matter more thoroughly, for my way with a number is legend." "Yes indeed," I agreed, "they've certainly chosen the right man." Homes and Gardens lit his pipe and

I sat back with a magazine. The rest of the flight was uneventful except for a slight altercation caused by some passengers who resented Homes and Gardens telling them how the movie ended before it even started ("Saw it at a screening last week," he confided to me triumphantly), but it was all soon settled and we arrived on schedule.

Precious Little had sent his matching car and driver and the ride to the hotel was a pleasant one. The Beverly Hills has in recent years lost a bit of its cachet, but Homes and Gardens is rather attached to its paging system and I myself am partial to its distinctive pink notepads.

No sooner had we settled into our bungalow (rather far from Halston's but right near the main building) than Precious himself arrived. "My Sher, my dear," he greeted us effusively and kissed us each on both cheeks, "you must come with me at once. That captain is becoming absolutely impossible. Daily his figures become more ridiculous and I have it from a very good source that he's hours away from talking to Rona."

"Well, well, Precious," said Homes and Gardens crisply, "that, of course, must be prevented, although it is unlikely, don't you think, that she'll take his call?" We all agreed and once more I was struck by Homes and Gardens's acute sensibilities.

The three of us got into the car—Homes and Gardens electing to sit up front, in order, he said, that he might see more clearly, although I imagine that what he wanted to see more clearly did not entirely exclude Juan, Precious's superbly café-au-lait driver. Homes and Gardens is, after all, a man of many interests.

We made an extensive tour of the various neighborhoods—Homes and Gardens gazing intently at every detail while Precious pointed out the homes of the stars. Our inspection completed, we repaired to Mr. Chow's, where we were welcomed extravagantly.

Precious and I looked at Homes and Gardens expectantly, but he avoided our eyes and I must confess that my heart sank as I allowed myself to feel for the very first time some doubt about my roommate. My spirits rose, however, when Homes and Gardens smiled precisely and said, "Oh, look, there's Liza, doesn't she look great?" I turned around and was pleased to see the celebrated entertainer waving cheerfully in our direction. We exchanged nods and turned our attention once again to Homes and Gardens, who was now obviously ready to address us.

"It's quite a simple thing really, reminds me in fact of the case involving the disappearance of a makeup artist at the *pret-à-porter* some years back. We knew for a fact that a makeup artist was missing—what we didn't know was just which makeup artist it was. Everyone, as you can imagine, was in a veritable tizzy, until I pointed out that we had only to examine the faces of the models, note which ones were most painfully lacking in cheekbone definition, inquire as to who did the makeup and thus we would have the name of the missing artist. From there the actual discovery of the young man took but a moment. Now, in the instance at hand, I must say we were most fortunate that the areas involved were not the very best, for had we been concerned with say, an area like Bel Air, we would have been confronted with the problem of ample household help. Since, however, we were dealing with such locales as Brentwood my work was quite trifling. You may have noticed, my dears, that I took much interest in the landscaping and I found exactly what I thought I would. A great many of the lawns were overgrown and needed cutting in the most dreadful way. I further learned that in many of the houses the garbage had not been taken out for days, nor had newspapers been delivered in quite some time. So many chores and part-time jobs left undone pointed to one thing and one thing only—that these neighborhoods were suffering from a dearth of underage boys. I simply counted up the amount of neglected work and can now present you with an accurate tally:

1,582 children under the age of fourteen are being exploited sexually in the Los Angeles area. 1,584, to be exact, but the other two are movie stars, which is, I regret, not illegal.

At least 10,000 local adult males actively pursue boys under the age of fourteen, but only 1,183 actually catch them.

8,000 juveniles from fourteen to seventeen years of age are used sexually by approximately 14,000 adult males (rather slim pickings, that) but 28,561 adult males are used to far greater advantage by 19,500 very crafty juveniles, many claiming to be from fourteen to seventeen years of age.

Homes and Gardens sat back with a satisfied air and Precious Little and I congratulated him heartily. Once again Homes and Gardens's admirable talents had triumphed, and on the way out of the restaurant we saw Barbra and Jon snubbing Kris.

Or Not CB:
That Is the Answer

It was with considerable approval that I listened one Sunday evening to my weekend host instruct his chauffeur to drive us, his guests, back to New York. The source of my approval was my firmly held conviction that public transportation should be avoided with precisely the same zeal that one accords Herpes II. And, I must say, in view of my slender means and broad acquaintance, I have on the whole, been remarkably successful in escaping both. It was, therefore, in excellent spirits that I settled myself comfortably in the back seat of the car. I smiled fondly at my companions, lit a cigarette, and entered enthusiastically into a discussion of the entertaining personal habits of those not present. Under such circumstances it is easily understandable that I did not, at first, pay much attention to what I innocently believed to be the harmless mutterings of the driver. It was not until a silence, afforded by a lull in the conversation, allowed me the opportunity of genuine eavesdropping that I became aware that someone was muttering back. I studied my fellow passengers and was much relieved to conclude that neither one had been concealing a secret knowledge of ventriloquism. That the chauffeur might possess such an intricate skill was quite out of the question. Overwhelmed by curiosity I asked him outright for an explanation. He replied that he was talking on the Citizen's Band radio he had recently installed in my host's automobile. The answering mutter was that of a truckdriver fifteen miles away. I asked him what he hoped to gain by this repartee. He replied that he was trading information on weather, traffic, and police radar cars.

I glanced out the window. It was a clear, starlit September evening. The traffic was bumper to bumper. If there was a police radar car in the vicinity it was probably reading the paper. I offered the chauffeur these observations. He responded by saying that he was finding out what the conditions were fifteen miles ahead of us. I replied that it was Sunday night, that we were on the Merritt Parkway bound for New York, and that ahead of us we would find the exact same conditions as those that currently prevailed except that they would become progressively more cosmopolitan. He ignored this news, preferring instead to resume his muttering. Seeing that this wasn't the first time I'd been thrown over for a truckdriver, I sat back to listen to what I imagined would be a distinctly lackluster conversation. What transpired, however, was unintelligible in a way I had not expected, for they spoke in a code that seemed totally devoid of meaning. This, I discovered, was CB slang—a special language used by those so inclined. As this was my first encounter with Citizen's Band radio, I feel justified in having responded with mere distaste. I knew nothing about it. Now more than a year has passed. I know a lot about it. And yes, I am appalled—yes, I am horrified—and yes, I take issue.

I originally planned to take issue in the form of an exchange of letters between Oscar Wilde and Lord Alfred Douglas written in CB slang. I labored diligently but with little success, for CB slang as a means of communication is irretrievably butch. It is, in fact, safe to say that if the population of the United States was relieved entirely of its girls and its male homosexuals, CB slang would be English.

I am eminently qualified to make this statement, as I studied intensively for the aforementioned project. Thus I am confident in my contention that when it comes to CB slang I am virtually fluent. This surprises me—for I carry with me the memory of a youth fairly teeming with French tutors, all of whom eventually admitted defeat and announced that I had no ear for language. Perhaps, perhaps, but it matters not, for it turns out that when it comes to *lingo* I've got an ear and a half. Clearly, my linguistic ability was not the problem. I did what I could. I assigned to Lord Douglas the CB "handle" (or nickname) of "Jailbait." For Mr. Wilde I chose "Jailbird," thereby achieving an enviable symmetry. I read scores of their real letters. I ground away at the CB dictionary. I tried full translations. I tried partial translations. I tried footnotes. To no avail. CB slang is, after all, a limited tongue concerned primarily with four-car collisions, radar traps, shifting gears, and stopping for coffee. Mr. Wilde's and Lord Douglas's thoughts were elsewhere. There are, for instance, no CB equivalents for the words "gilt," "narcissus," "insouciance," or "honey-haired boy." And even the most perfect epigram suffers when interpreted in a language that refers to a bed as a "snore shelf."

Fortunately, I am a plucky sort and more than willing to express my displeasure in another manner:

The very word *citizen* implies a preoccupation with democracy that cannot help but be construed as fanatical. And not without reason, for entree to the world of

CB is wide open to all and sundry—particularly all. It is harder, I assure you, to get into Macy's.

*   *   *

To the average (and you will look long and hard before finding anyone so aptly described) CB aficionado his radio is his hobby. A hobby is, of course, an abomination, as are all consuming interests and passions that do not lead directly to large, personal gain.

*   *   *

CB radio is a common bond. Any bond that cannot, upon demand of the bearer, be converted immediately into cash is sorely deficient in both refinement and dignity.

*   *   *

CB slang is on the one hand too colorful and on the other hand lacking a counterpart for the words *pearl gray*.

*   *   *

Citizen's Band radio renders one accessible to a wide variety of people from all walks of life. It should not be forgotten that all walks of life include conceptual artists, dry cleaners, and living poets.

*   *   *

CB communication consists almost wholly of actual information. It is, therefore, of no interest to the civilized conversationalist.

The Word *Lady:*
Most Often Used to Describe Someone You Wouldn't Want to Talk to for Even Five Minutes

For years and years people who had them referred to their girl friends as their girl friends. With the advent of that unattractive style known as hip, many people stole the term *old lady* from perfectly innocent black jazz musicians and began using it in regard to their own girl friends. Then came women's lib and quite a number of people apparently felt that the word *old* was sexist. These people began to call their girl friends their "ladies."

Lest you get the impression that I am totally opposed to the word *lady* I rush to assure you that I think it is a perfectly nice word when used correctly. The word *lady* is used correctly only as follows:

A. To refer to certain female members of the English aristocracy.

B. In reference to girls who stand behind lingerie counters in department stores, but only when preceded by the word *sales.*

C. To alert a member of the gentle sex to the fact that she is no longer playing with a full deck. As in, "Lady, what are you—nuts or something?"

D. To differentiate between girls who put out and girls who don't. Girls who put out are tramps. Girls who don't are ladies. This is, however, a rather archaic usage of the word. Should one of you boys happen upon a girl who doesn't put out, do not jump to the conclusion that you have found a lady. What you have probably found is a lesbian.

Taking a Letter

As one with a distinct aversion to newspapers I rely heavily for information on the random remarks of others. Therefore my sources are far from impeccable. They are, however, not without a peculiar whimsical charm all their own and thus not to be taken lightly. For example, I was recently informed that the United States Postal Service was considering cutting its deliveries down to three days a week. The informant was a source close to his mother and therefore reliable. My immediate reaction was one of shock and dismay until I remembered that in my neighborhood a week that sees three whole mail deliveries is a thing rare and precious. I began to wonder why it was that my local mail service was so far ahead of that of the rest of the nation and decided to make discreet inquiries.

My neighborhood is located in Greenwich Village, a quarter of the city well known for its interesting artistic qualities. These qualities are to be found not only in its atmosphere and residents but also in its public servants. There is, in fact, not a single local postal employee who does not possess a temperament of such lush moodiness that one assumes that only an unfortunate lack of rhythm has kept them from careers devoted to the composition of tragic opera. Exhaustive research soon established that this was no accident but a carefully planned effort to bring the post office closer to those it serves. The Greenwich Village Postal System is a separate entity dedicated to the proposition that nowhere on earth are men created more equal than downtown on the West Side. Thus its offices exhibit a clean Bauhaus influence. The wanted posters refer to desires more personal than federal. Uniforms are chosen on the basis of cut and fabric. And they have punched up the official motto with the Greenwich Village Addendum so that it reads as follows: "Neither snow nor rain nor heat nor gloom of night can stay these couriers from swift completion of their appointed rounds. *However,* offended sensibility, painful memory, postman's block, and previous engagements may stay the courier for an indefinite period of time. *C'est la vie.*" Closer examination of this motto reveals these inner truths:

Offended Sensibility

A Situation of Offended Sensibility is declared when an assigned route contains the following:

1. Architecture of unpleasant proportion.
2. An excessive number of conceptual artists. The official definition of "excessive" in such cases is stated as "More than two if dead, more than one if alive."
3. Musicians who are awake.
4. Dandyish house pets.
5. Ethnic restaurants featuring interesting food.

Painful Memory

A Situation of Painful Memory can be invoked when a courier is called upon to deliver mail to districts in which:

1. He has had an emotionally satisfactory but physically crippling sexual encounter.

2. He consumed a carelessly prepared shrimp curry.
3. He was snubbed.

Postman's Block

Postman's Block is a virulent condition that attacks the more sensitive couriers with alarming regularity. Its symptoms are:

1. The inability to find the right address caused by an inhibiting perfectionism and a belief that the right address—that big address that you always thought you had in you—shall ever elude your grasp.
2. A tendency to misread zip codes coupled with the nagging doubt that they are perhaps not as zippy as all that.
3. A conviction that you are burnt out. That your great days of swift completion are behind you.

Previous Engagements

The Greenwich Village postman does his best to keep his working hours free but he is, of course, not immune to the killing pace of urban life and frequently discovers that he's booked up pretty solid. This is not surprising since he is a firm believer in the adage "finders keepers" and so is caught up in the dizzying whirl that is the social and business life of others. A look at a page from his appointment calendar reveals the following:

Mardi 6 avril

10:30— Attend board meeting, Ford Foundation
12:00— Conference with agent to discuss Dutch translation
1:00— Lunch, La Côte Basque—Barbara Walters
3:30— Address meeting of United Nations Security Council
6:00— Fashion Show, 500 Club—Stephen Burrows—ready-to-wear
8:00— Screening at Paramount
10:00— Working dinner—Jonas Salk—Orsini's

Writers on Strike:
A Chilling Prophecy

Major cities are not infrequently afflicted with strikes
and demonstrations by doctors, garbagemen, firemen,
and police. There is always a public outcry, as those
concerned with public safety are quick to envision a city
full of burning garbage and contagious murderers.
However, garbage in the street, flames in the bedroom,
killers on the loose, and spots on the lungs are merely
physical inconveniences. Far more serious work stop-
pages can occur, and politicians and citizens confronted
with the more traditional problems can comfort themselves with the thought "Well, it's a hell of a mess but
thank God it's not the writers." Because, believe you me,
compared to the writers even the Teamsters are a piece
of cake.

Imagine, if you will, a rainy Sunday afternoon in New
York. All over town, writers are lying in bed, their heads
under their respective pillows. They are of varying
heights and builds, races, religions, and creeds, but they
are as one: whining. Some of them are whining to themselves. Some to companions. It matters not in the least.
Simultaneously they all turn over and reach for the

phone. In a matter of seconds every writer in New York is speaking to another writer in New York. They are talking about not writing. This is, next to who's not queer, perhaps the most popular topic of discussion among writers in New York. Ordinarily there are variations on this theme and one reacts accordingly:

Variation on This Theme Number One

You can't write. You call another writer. He can't write, either. This is terrific. You can now talk about not writing for two hours and then go out to dinner with each other until four o'clock in the morning.

Variation on This Theme Number Two

You can't write. You call another writer. He is writing. *This* is a great tragedy. He will talk to you only as long as it takes for him to impress upon you the fact that not only is he writing but he thinks that *what* he is writing is quite possibly the best thing he's ever written. Your only alternative to suicide in this situation is to call a rock musician. This makes you feel smart again and you can get on with the business of not writing.

Variation on This Theme Number Three

You are writing. Another writer calls you to talk about not writing. You announce that you *are.* Masochistically he inquires as to what it is that you are writing. You inform him modestly that it's just a little something vaguely reminiscent of, say, *An Ideal Husband,* perhaps a bit funnier. Your behavior at his funeral the following day is marked by enormous dignity and grace.

There are other variations on this theme but I think you get my drift. Now, on this particular Sunday afternoon a phenomenon has occurred. Every single writer in the city of New York is not writing. Once knowledge of this has spread throughout the entire non-writing writing community, a tremendous feeling of mutual relief and well-being is experienced. For an exquisite moment all the writers in New York like each other. If *no one* can write, then it is obviously not the fault of the writers. It must be *their* fault. The writers band together. They will have their revenge on the city. No longer will they lie abed not writing in the privacy of their own homes. They will not write publicly. They will go on strike. They decide to stage a sitdown in the lobby of the Algonquin Hotel and not write there.

It takes a while but about a year and a half later people begin to notice that there's nothing to read. First they notice that the newsstands are quite empty. Then it begins to get television news coverage. There is still television news, mostly lip sync—some ad lib. People begin to get annoyed. They demand that the city take steps. The city assembles a group to go in and negotiate with the writers. The group consists of a fireman, a doctor, a sanitationman, and a policeman. The writers refuse to negotiate. Their reply to a city on its knees? "Call my agent." The agents refuse to negotiate until they can figure out a way to sell the movie rights. The strike continues. The Red Cross is allowed to cross the picket lines to dispense royalty statements and cappucino. The situation becomes more desperate. Adults all over the country are sitting in bus stations playing jacks. Old copies of *People* magazine are auctioned off and sold at Parke-Bernet for incredible prices. Librarians begin to take bribes and are seen driving lavender Cadillacs with quilted vinyl roofs and page-shaped rear windows. A syndicate is formed by a group who own several back issues of *The New Yorker*. They open a membership-only after-hours reading bar, which is fire-bombed by a radical organization that believes that Donald Barthelme belongs to the people.

Finally the National Guard is called in. Hundreds of heavily armed Guardsmen arrive at the Algonquin. They are forced to retreat under a stinging barrage of sarcastic remarks.

Although the writers have agreed not to have a leader, one of their members becomes something of an authority figure. His influence is based largely on the fact that he has on his person a hardcover copy of *Gravity's Rainbow,* which he is widely believed to have read in its entirety. In reality he is a disguised labor mediator sent by the city to infiltrate the writers and break the strike. He is insidious and stealthily goes about convincing writers that other writers are secretly writing and will have actual manuscripts completed and ready for publication when the strike ends. He does his work well. The writers leave the Algonquin and go back to not writing at home. When they realize they have been duped, and by whom, they are near-suicidal at their lack of perception. So, then, let this be a lesson to you all: never judge a cover by its book.

A Few Words
on a Few Words

Democracy is an interesting, even laudable, notion and there is no question but that when compared to Communism, which is too dull, or Fascism, which is too exciting, it emerges as the most palatable form of government. This is not to say that it is without its drawbacks—chief among them being its regrettable tendency to encourage people in the belief that all men are created equal. And although the vast majority need only take a quick look around the room to see that this is hardly the case, a great many remain utterly convinced.

The major problem resulting from this conviction is that it causes such people to take personally the inalienable right of freedom of speech. This in itself would be at least tolerable were this group not given to such a broad interpretation of the word *freedom* or such a slender interpretation of the word *speech*.

It would further ameliorate the situation were these equality buffs to recall that one of the distinguishing characteristics of democracy is the division between the public sector and the private sector. The founding fathers may have had any number of things in mind when they made this admirable distinction, but surely their primary consideration was to protect the articulate against the possibility of overhearing the annoying conversation of others.

Since the Bill of Rights in its present form leaves far too much to the imagination, it is obviously necessary for some sane, responsible citizen to step forward and explain in detail just exactly what is meant by freedom of speech. Being as civic-minded as the next girl, I willingly accept this challenge. Lest you assume that I possess unreasonable and dangerous dictatorial impulses, I assure you that my desire to curtail undue freedom of speech extends only to such public arenas as restaurants, airports, streets, hotel lobbies, parks, and department stores. Verbal exchanges between consenting adults in private are of as little interest to me as they probably are to them. I wish only to defend the impressionable young and the fastidious old against the ravages of unseemly word usage. To this end I have prepared a list of words which should be used in public only as specified.

1. *art*—This word may be publicly used in only two instances:
   A. As a nickname—in which case the suffix *ie* may be added to form the word *Artie*.
   B. By a native of the East End of London to describe a vital organ, as in the sentence, "Blimy, I feel poorly —must be my bleedin' 'art."
2. *love*—The word *love* may be used in public only to refer to inanimate or totally inaccessible objects.
   A. "I love linguini with clam sauce" is always acceptable.
   B. "I love Truman Capote" is acceptable only if one is not personally acquainted with him. If one is personally acquainted with Mr. Capote it is rather unlikely at this time that one would be moved to express such a sentiment.

3. *relationship*—The civilized conversationalist uses this word in public only to describe a seafaring vessel carrying members of his family.

4. *diaphragm*—Public decency demands that this word be used only to refer to the midriff area of the body and then only by doctors—never by singers.

5. *Ms.*—The wise avoid this word entirely but:
   A. It may be used on paper by harried members of the publishing world who find it necessary to abbreviate the word manuscript.
   B. Or by native residents of the south and southwestern portions of the United States as follows: "I sho do ms. that purty little gal."

6. *honest*—This word is suitable for public use only to indicate extreme distaste, as in the sentence "Dorothy has become absolutely unbearable—I think she must be on est."

7. *internalize*—To be used (if at all) only to describe that process by which a formerly harmless medical student becomes a menace to the sick and helpless.

8. *fair*—This word is to be used only in reference to a carnival-type event and not as an expression of justice —for not only is such usage unpleasant but also, I assure you, quite useless.

9. *assert*—One would do well to remember that as far as public utterance is concerned, *assert* refers only to that which is two mints in one.

No News Is Preferable

For some it's the columns, for others the logic, but for
me when it comes to the most winning aspect of
Greek culture I'll take the killing of the bearer of bad
news. Throw in the bearer of good news and you've
got yourself a practice that's nothing short of perfect.
And one, I should like to point out, that would make
a welcome addition to any culture, particularly one
such as our own. I am, of course, well aware that
many people *like* the news—that they consider it to
be important, informative, even entertaining. To
these people I can only say: You're wrong. Not that I
wish to be curt with you—not at all. I am perfectly
willing to elaborate. In order that you might more
fully understand the error of your ways, let us consider each alleged attribute separately.

Important

When dealing with a concept such as *important* one
would be well advised to ask: "To whom?" In this way

we can more directly attack the problem. And almost immediately we can see that the "whom" is probably not us. We arrive at this conclusion by asking of ourselves the following questions:

1. Before going to work do I don a highly colored blazer the pocket of which is adorned with a number?
2. Once so attired, do I sit down at a long, curved counter and make jokes with old athletes and minority-group women?
3. Do I periodically interrupt this repartee to look into a camera and relate in an authoritative yet warm tone of voice the unpleasant activities of unattractive people?
4. Do I number among my colleagues at least one who has made a career for herself out of dressing up as a mother and buying dangerous household products?

If our answers to these questions are nos, then I think we can agree that when it comes to the news, "important" is not an appropriate adjective. Unless, of course, you earn your living by delivering papers on a bicycle, in which case the news *is* important but only when compared to you.

Informative

Strictly speaking, the news *is* informative insofar as it does indeed provide information. Therefore the questions one must ask here are:

1. Do I want this information?
2. Do I need this information?
3. What do they expect me to do about it?

Answer to Question Number One

No. If a genetically handicapped Scientologist attempts to take the life of the vice-president of the 4H

Clubs of Texas with a crossbow and someone knows about it, I would prefer that he kept it to himself.

Answer to Question Number Two

No. If three unemployed psychopathic blacksmiths have stolen the daughter of the inventor of lead paint and are threatening to read to her aloud from *Fear of Flying* until everyone in Marin County is given a horse, I fail to see how knowing this will help me to find a large but inexpensive apartment in a better neighborhood.

Answer to Question Number Three

I cannot possibly imagine.

Entertaining

In researching this subject I watched a fair amount of television news and read a couple of papers. I didn't laugh once.

In the interest of fair play I offer two news situations that I find acceptable. One exists. The other does not. Naturally the one that exists is not nearly as acceptable as the one that does not. And this is probably as good a definition of reality as you are likely to find.

Radio News

Radio news is bearable. This is due to the fact that while the news is being broadcast the disc jockey is not allowed to talk.

Personalized News

Walter Cronkite appears on the screen. He fixes you with a weighty yet good-humored gaze. The whisper of a smile plays around the corners of his forthright mouth. He begins. "Good evening, Fran. While you were lying on the couch today rereading old copies of English *Vogue* and drinking Perrier water your book wrote itself. All indications are that it's perfect. A source close to *The New York Times Book Review* called it 'splendid, brilliantly funny, a surefire hit.' A reputable Hollywood authority—yes, Fran, we found one just for you—reports cutthroat bidding for the movie rights and many in the industry fear that it will set a dangerously high precedent. On the home front, Lauren Bacall called a press conference this afternoon to announce that she wants to trade apartments with you and an informed expert leaked the information that all of the conceptual artists in New York are moving to East Berlin. Well, Fran, that about wraps it up for now. See you tomorrow night, when things will be even better."

Social Studies

People

People

P eople (a group that in my opinion has always attracted an undue amount of attention) have often
been likened to snowflakes. This analogy is meant to suggest
that each is unique—no two alike. This is quite patently not
the case. People, even at the current rate of inflation—in
fact, people especially at the current rate of inflation—are
quite simply a dime a dozen. And, I hasten to add, their only
similarity to snowflakes resides in their invariable and lamentable tendency to turn, after a few warm days, to slush.

This is, I am aware, though not a particularly popular
sentiment, also not exactly a novel one either. I do believe,
however, that this is the very first time it has ever been
expressed with an intention to substantiate it with well-
documented written evidence. In other words, everybody
talks about people but nobody ever does anything about
them.

What I have decided to do about them is to point out that
except in extremely rare instances people are pretty much
like everyone else. They all say the same things, have the
same names and wear their hair in the same styles. This is
not a modern phenomenon but one that has been true

throughout all of history. This can clearly be seen in the following orderly fashion:

I. WHAT PEOPLE SAY

Below you will find the complete and unabridged record of the general conversation of the general public since time immemorial:

 a. Hi, how are you?
 b. I did not.
 c. Good. Now you know how I felt.
 d. Do you mind if I go ahead of you? I only have this one thing.

II. WHAT PEOPLE ARE CALLED

This varies from era to era but at any given time almost everyone has the same name. Your average Joe has simply become your average Jennifer. In more ways than one.

III. HOW PEOPLE WEAR THEIR HAIR

When it comes to hair, the possibilities are not, fortunately, endless. And while this may be news to sportscasters and hairdressers, it is nevertheless a fact. The evidence is overwhelmingly conclusive and this list proves it.

People Who Have or Have Had Almost
the Exact Same Hairstyle
 a. Victor Hugo and Sarah Caldwell
 b. William Wordsworth and Frank Lloyd Wright

c. W. B. Yeats and David Hockney
d. Jean Cocteau and Eli Wallach
e. Johan August Strindberg and Katharine Hepburn
f. Pablo Picasso and my maternal grandfather, Phillip Splaver

All of the above is true; and if you don't believe me, you can look it up for yourself.

Now that we have learned these elementary lessons, most of you are probably asking yourselves the question, "Well, then, in what ways *do* people differ from one another?" There are two answers to this question. First of all, everyone has a different—and yes, even unique—size foot. In fact, no two feet are exactly alike—not even, as you have probably discovered, your own two feet. Every single human foot has its own inimitable size, its own distinctive shape, its own little personality. *Feet* are like snowflakes. Your feet, more than anything else, are what make you you, and nobody else's are quite like them.

The second thing that distinguishes you, sets you apart from the crowd, is that everybody in the entire world likes his eggs done a different and special way. When it comes to eggs, everyone has his own subtle preference, his own individual taste. So the next time that someone asks you how you like your eggs, speak right up. After all, you only go around once.

It is at this juncture that many of you may now be thinking that the state of affairs thus far described is a sorry one indeed. Wouldn't things be a whole lot better, you may be asking, if, say, egg preferences were uniform but conversation somewhat more varied? Yes, things certainly would be a whole lot better, and yet, although there is a solution to this problem, it is one that could only be brought about by the greatest mutual effort. The solution is this: I will supply a short course in conversational uplift if you will all decide on one universal way you like your eggs. I realize, of course, that it will be difficult for such a diverse and colorful group of foot sizes to come to such an agreement, but if you promise to at least try, I too will do my best.

Before we tackle the larger and more comprehensive issues of conversation, I feel that a few words on the subject of trying too hard might well be in order.

Trying Too Hard

The conversational overachiever is someone whose grasp exceeds his reach. This is possible but not attractive.

———

Original thought is like original sin: both happened before you were born to people you could not possibly have met.

———

The Larger and More Comprehensive Issues

Great people talk about ideas, average people talk about things, and small people talk about wine.

———

Polite conversation is rarely either.

———

Spilling your guts is just exactly as charming as it sounds.

———

Never name-drop at the dinner table. The only thing worse than a fly in one's soup is a celebrity.

———

The only appropriate reply to the question "Can I be frank?" is "Yes, if I can be Barbara."

———

Telling someone he looks healthy isn't a compliment—it's a second opinion.

———

Looking genuinely attentive is like sawing a girl in half and then putting her back together. It is seldom achieved without the use of mirrors.

———

The opposite of talking isn't listening. The opposite of talking is waiting.

———

Hot Not to Marry
a Millionaire:
A Guide for the
Misfortune Hunter

The recent marriage of a well-known Greek shipping heiress and an unemployed Russian Communist has given rise to the speculation that we may, in fact, be witnessing an incipient trend. It is not unlikely that working your way down may shortly become the romantic vogue among the truly rich—with interest ranging from the merely less fortunate to the genuinely poor. Should this become the case, our more affluent brethren will undoubtedly be in need of some practical advice and careful guidance. Thus I offer the following course of instruction:

I. WHERE POORER PEOPLE CONGREGATE

Meeting the poorer person is a problem in itself, for the more conventional avenues of acquaintance are closed to you. The poorer person did not prep with your brother, form a racehorse syndicate with your broker or lose to you gracefully in Deauville. He does not share your aesthetic interest in pre-Columbian jewelry, your childhood passion for teasing the cook or your knowledge of land values in Gstaad. Therefore, it is not probable that the poorer person is someone whom you are just going to run into by chance. He must be actively sought. In seeking the poorer person, one must be ever mindful of both his habits and his daily routine:

a. The very backbone of the mass-transit system *is* the poorer person, who when he must go somewhere will usually avail himself of the vivid camaraderie to be found on buses and subways. Should you choose this method, take special care that you do not give yourself away by an awkward and superfluous attempt to hail the E train or by referring to the bus driver as "the captain."

b. The poorer person performs most personal services for himself. Thus he can commonly be found in the acts of purchasing food, laundering clothing, shopping for hardware, picking up prescriptions and returning empty bottles. These tasks can be accomplished at locations throughout the city and are all open to the public, which can, if you like, include yourself.

c.   Generally speaking, the poorer person summers
     where he winters.

d.   Unless he's an extremely poorer person (i.e., a welfare
     recipient) he will spend a substantial portion of each
     day or night at work. Work may occur in any number
     of places: stores, offices, restaurants, houses, airports
     or the front seats of taxicabs. With the possible ex-
     ception of the last, you yourself have easy and fre-
     quent access to all such locales—a circumstance that
     can often be used to advantage, as it affords you the
     opportunity of making that crucial first gesture.

II. BREAKING THE ICE WITH POORER PEOPLE

In approaching the poorer person, one can employ, of
course, the same tactics that one might use in approaching
someone on more equal footing with oneself. Charm, wit,
tact, direct eye contact, simple human warmth, the feigning
of interest in his deeper feelings—all of these may be beneficial in establishing rapport. Such strategies are, however, not
without risk, for they are every one open to misinterpreta-
tion and most certainly cannot be counted upon for immediate results. Poorer people, being, alas, not only poorer but
also people, are quirky; they too have their little moods, their
sore spots, their prickly defenses. Therefore their responses
to any of the above might well be erratic and not quite all
that one has hoped. Do not lose heart, though, for it is here
that your own position as a richer person can best be exploited and can, in fact, assure you of almost instantaneous
success in getting to know the poorer person more inti-
mately.

Buy the poorer person an expensive present: a car; a house; a color television set; a dining-room table. Something nice. The poorer person, without exception, loves all these things. Buy him one of them and he will definitely like you enough to at least chat.

III. WHAT NOT TO SAY TO POORER PEOPLE

It is at this juncture that the utmost care be exercised lest you lose your hard-won toehold. For it is in actual conversation with the poorer person that even the most attentive and conscientious student tends to falter.

Having been softened up with a lavish gift, the poorer person will indeed be in an expansive, even friendly, frame of mind. He is not, however, completely and irrevocably yours yet; it is still possible to raise his hackles and make as naught all of your previous efforts. A thoughtless remark, an inopportune question, an unsuitable reference—any of these may offend the poorer person to the point where you may totally alienate him. Below are some examples of the sort of thing one really must strive to avoid:

a. Is that your blue Daimler blocking the driveway?

b. . . . and in the end, of course, it's always the larger stockholder who is blamed.

c. I'll call you around noon. Will you be up?

d. Who do you think you are, anyway—Lucius Beebe?

e. Don't you believe it for a minute—these waiters make an absolute fortune.

f. Oh, a uniform. What a great idea.

IV. A SHORT GLOSSARY OF WORDS USED BY POORER
PEOPLE

sale—An event common to the retail business, during the
course of which merchandise is reduced in price. Not to
be confused with *sail,* which is, at any rate, a good word
not to say to poorer people.

meatloaf—A marvelously rough kind of pâté. Sometimes
served hot.

overworked—An overwhelming feeling of fatigue; exhaus-
tion; weariness. Similar to jet lag.

rent—A waste of money. It's so much cheaper to buy.

The Four
Greediest Cases:
A Limited Appeal

Angela de G.

I t is quiet now in the almost devastated East River co-op. Tarps litter the seriously marred parquet floors. Paint-stained ladders stand like skeletons in the somber dimness of insufficient track lighting. Abandoned shades of gray sadly spot a lower wall. Forlorn swatches of fabric in a harsh jumble of acid greens and impenetrable blacks are strewn angrily across a veritable ruin of an Empire Récamier. It is quiet now. Yes. Now. But for Angela de G., the occupant of this cavernous wreck, the momentary quiet is but an all too brief interlude. A precious chunk of serenity in a world that has turned upside down. A world made chaotic and unsure. A world of terror and bleakness. A world of despair.

Angela de G. is renovating.

Quietly the small figure sits huddled in a huge coffee-colored sweater that is much too big for her emaciated frame. A sweater so voluminous and ill-fitting that one can barely hear her speak—a sweater, alas, that she could hardly refuse no matter how wretched the cut, how unflattering the hue, how inappropriate the garment to her way of life.

It was a gift from the designer.

But Angela de G., as she stares out the window, across the freezing black river and into the bleakness of Queens, seems oblivious to her attire. So great is her present crisis, so encompassing her depression that it is almost—almost—as if even clothes didn't matter any more.

As Angela de G. talks, one is immediately struck by the conflict in her voice—low in volume but loud in agony as she pours out her litany of despair—a tale all too familiar to those of us in the social services. Familiar, yes, but nonetheless heartrending, for Angela de G.'s pain is real, her burden heavy. So one listens and one hears. Hears it all—the bitter fighting between the decorator and the architect, the arrogance of the lighting designer, the workmen who are late, the painters who are clumsy. The time and a half, the double time, the shock of hitherto unconsidered legal holidays. Yes, one listens, one hears, and one does, of course, what little one can. Hesitantly, all too aware of the meagerness of one's assistance, the terrible inadequacy of one's own ability to cope with such a situation, one offers what is, after all, cold comfort. The name of a little man marvelous with parquet. The number of a non-union plumber in Newark. The hope that she will someday find an upholsterer who knows what he's doing. Yes, one tries. One makes an effort, puts up a good front. But one knows, finally, that it will take more. That outside aid is needed. And needed badly.

Angela de G. is renovating.

Won't you please help?

Leonard S.

Leonard S. is alone. Very alone. All alone. Yes, Leonard S. is by himself now. It was not always this way. Once it was different. Quite different. Last night, in fact. But all that has changed now. All that is over. For this morning, when Leonard S. awoke, he was confronted head-on with a tragedy he had long been dreading. Christopher R. was gone. Yes, Christopher R., dear, sweet, beautifully proportioned Christopher R. had left and Leonard S. was alone. Christopher R., however, was not alone. He was with all of Leonard S.'s cash, half of Leonard S.'s wardrobe, Leonard S.'s portable color television set, and Leonard S.'s exquisite little Ingres drawing.

Leonard S. hopes Christopher R. is happy now.

Happy with the way he's treated Leonard S. Happy with the lies, the deceptions, the cheating. Happy with the way he's hustled Leonard S.—used his connections, his credit-card number, his account at Paul Stuart's. Happy with his adolescent arrogance, happy with his unspeakable ingratitude, happy with his exquisite little Ingres drawing.

Leonard S. is not happy. He is depressed. He is sick and he is tired. He is headachey. His illusions are shattered. His trust has been violated. He doesn't feel like going to work. He is a broken man like a million other broken men in a cold, unfeeling city. He is unbearably low. He is suffused with gloom. And he just can't face the studio today.

Leonard S. talks, and his pain is a terrible thing to witness. Leonard S. loved Christopher R. Cherished him, cared for him, supported him. Leonard S. thought Christopher R. was loyal. Thought he was decent, thought he was different. Different from the others. Different from Timothy M., John H., Rodney W., David T., Alexander J., Matthew C., Benjamin P. and Joseph K. Different from Ronald B., from Anthony L. and from Carl P. But he was wrong. Very wrong.

He sees that now.

He must have been blind. He must have been crazy. He must have been out of his mind.

The phone rings.

Leonard S. returns from the call and it is apparent that tragedy has struck again. He pours himself a drink. His hands shake. His eyes are twin pools of anguish. He can barely speak, but slowly the sordid story is told. He has been doubly betrayed. What little faith he had left has deserted him completely. Christopher R. is en route to Los Angeles. With Leonard S.'s heart. With all of Leonard S.'s cash. With half of Leonard S.'s wardrobe. With Leonard S.'s portable color television set. With Leonard S.'s exquisite little Ingres drawing.

And with Leonard S.'s assistant, Michael F.

Leonard S. says he is through. He says he is finished. He says nothing means anything to him anymore—nothing at all. But perhaps there is yet some hope. Perhaps *you* can help. All contributions are in the strictest confidence. Anonymity is assured. We dare not speak your last name.

Mr. and Mrs. Alan T.

There was laughter here once. Music too. Parties. Celebrations. Catering.

Fun.

But now this Tudor-style home in Bel Air is tense. Those that live here are worn. Nervous. They are doing their best, but the pressure is intolerable, the demands not to be believed. They are suffering the agonizing results of bad judgment. Faulty figuring. Sour deals.

They have misread the general public.

There was a time when that seemed impossible. When Mr. and Mrs. Alan T. were riding high. The smartest, the sharpest producing and packaging team in town. Sure-footed, never faltering, never a mistake. Residuals, big box office, percentages of the gross, not the net. It all belonged to Mr. and Mrs. Alan T. Their respective fingers on the pulse of America. Mr. and Mrs. Right Place at the Right Time. There with the goods. Disaffected youth when America wanted disaffected youth. Black exploitation. Nostalgia. Male bonding. The occult. They predicted every single trend. Right on the money. Time after time. They had contacts. They had respect. They had power. They had four brand-new leased Mercedes all at once. Chocolate brown. Off-white. Silver gray. Deepest maroon. All paid for, compliments of the studio.

Then it all started caving in on them. A mistake here, an error there. Little things at first: going into general release too soon; giving a twenty-year-old director a budget he couldn't handle; using an editor with a drinking problem;

putting a cute little number in a role that swamped her. Bad reviews. Drive-in city.

The maroon was the first to go. Then the off-white. Mr. and Mrs. Alan T. live with the sort of despair that few of us can truly understand. They are like wounded deer, like victims of some corrosive disease of the soul. They sit and stare at each other in mournful silence. They know it is only a matter of time. They know the silver gray is next. Then even the chocolate brown will be gone. They castigate themselves and each other. Their plight is all the harder to bear, for these once proud people see it as a failing of their own. An unrelenting self-induced horror.

Mr. and Mrs. Alan T. missed the boat on science fiction. How it happened they simply cannot imagine. All the signs were there: paperbacks selling like hotcakes; huge conventions of future buffs; comic books; toys. A trend about to be. A gold mine. A money machine. A whole new ball game. And where were they? They answer their own question with a horrifying combination of grief and self-loathing. Off on location with some bomb about a Yorkshire terrier possessed by the devil. Yesterday's newspapers, January's Playmate of the Month in February.

Can you come to their aid? Can you help Mr. and Mrs. Alan T.? Try. Please. Make them an offer. They can hardly refuse. Can they?

Kimberly M.

Kimberly M. stands alone in the airline terminal. A solitary figure. Staring as the empty luggage carrousel goes round and round. She knows it is to no avail. She has been there for hours. She has waited. She has talked to them all: the representatives, the ground crew, even, in her blinding panic, the stewardesses. She has had her hopes lifted only to be dashed. Her luggage, she knows, is gone. All seven pieces. All a gift from her grandmother. All Louis Vuitton. All the old stuff. The real stuff.

When it was still leather.

She cannot quite believe this is happening to *her*. It must be some dreadful nightmare from which she will soon awake. It cannot be real. But as Kimberly M. hears the metallic voice announcing the delays and cancellations, she knows this is no hallucination, no dream. They have indeed lost her luggage. Where it is she hasn't a clue. Taken by mistake? In a taxi on its way back to town? En route to Cleveland? Checked through to Hong Kong? She may never know.

Gone, her Sonia Rykiel sweaters. Her favorite Kenzo shirt. Gone, her new supply of Clinique. Her Maud Frizon shoes. Gone, her Charles Jourdan boots. Gone, her address book. Yes. Her address book. Gone. Gone. Gone.

Kimberly M. stands alone in the airline terminal. A solitary figure. Staring as the empty luggage carrousel goes round and round.

Kimberly M. has lost her luggage. Certainly you can spare some of your own.

REMEMBER THE GREEDIEST!

Parental Guidance

As the title suggests, this piece is intended for those among us who have taken on the job of human reproduction. And while I am not unmindful of the fact that many of my readers are familiar with the act of reproduction only insofar as it applies to a too-recently fabricated Louis XV armoire, I nevertheless feel that certain things cannot be left unsaid. For although distinctly childless myself, I find that I am possessed of some fairly strong opinions on the subject of the rearing of the young. The reasons for this are varied, not to say rococo, and range from genuine concern for the future of mankind to simple, cosmetic disdain.

Being a good deal less villainous than is popularly supposed, I do not hold small children entirely accountable for their own behavior. By and large, I feel that this burden must be borne by their elders. Therefore, in an effort to make knowledge power, I offer the following suggestions:

Your responsibility as a parent is not as great as you might imagine. You need not supply the world with the next conqueror of disease or major motion-picture star. If your child simply grows up to be someone who does not use the word "collectible" as a noun, you can consider yourself an unqualified success.

––––––

Children do not really need money. After all, they don't have to pay rent or send mailgrams. Therefore their allowance should be just large enough to cover chewing gum and an occasional pack of cigarettes. A child with his own savings account and/or tax shelter is not going to be a child who scares easy.

––––––

A child who is not rigorously instructed in the matter of table manners is a child whose future is being dealt with cavalierly. A person who makes an admiral's hat out of a linen napkin is not going to be in wild social demand.

––––––

The term "child actor" is redundant. He should not be further incited.

––––––

Do not have your child's hair cut by a real hairdresser in a real hairdressing salon. He is, at this point, far too short to be exposed to contempt.

––––––

Do not, on a rainy day, ask your child what he feels like doing, because I assure you that what he feels like doing, you won't feel like watching.

––––––

Educational television should be absolutely forbidden. It can only lead to unreasonable expectations and eventual disappointment when your child discovers that the letters of the alphabet do not leap up out of books and dance around the room with royal-blue chickens.

———

If you are truly serious about preparing your child for the future, don't teach him to subtract—teach him to deduct.

———

Make every effort to avoid ostentatiously Biblical names. Nothing will show your hand more.

———

Do not send your child to the sort of progressive school that permits writing on the walls unless you want him to grow up to be TAKI 183.

———

If you must give your child lessons, send him to driving school. He is far more likely to end up owning a Datsun than he is a Stradivarius.

———

Designer clothes worn by children are like snowsuits worn by adults. Few can carry it off successfully.

———

Never allow your child to call you by your first name. He hasn't known you long enough.

———

Do not encourage your child to express himself artistically unless you are George Balanchine's mother.

———

Do not elicit your child's political opinions. He doesn't know any more than you do.

———

Do not allow your children to mix drinks. It is unseemly and they use too much vermouth.

———

Letting your child choose his own bedroom furniture is like letting your dog choose his own veterinarian.

––––––

Your child is watching too much television if there exists the possibility that he might melt down.

––––––

Don't bother discussing sex with small children. They rarely have anything to add.

––––––

Never, for effect, pull a gun on a small child. He won't get it.

––––––

Ask your child what he wants for dinner only if he's buying.

––––––

Tips for Teens

There is perhaps, for all concerned, no period of life so unpleasant, so unappealing, so downright unpalatable, as that of adolescence. And while pretty much everyone who comes into contact with him is disagreeably affected, certainly no one is in for a ruder shock than the actual teenager himself. Fresh from twelve straight years of uninterrupted cuteness, he is singularly unprepared to deal with the harsh consequences of inadequate personal appearance. Almost immediately upon entering the thirteenth year of life, a chubby little child becomes a big fat girl, and a boy previously spoken of as "small for his age" finds that he is, in reality, a boy who is short.

Problems of physical beauty, grave though they be, are not all that beset the unwary teen. Philosophical, spiritual, social, legal—a veritable multitude of difficulties daily confront him. Understandably disconcerted, the teenager almost invariably finds himself in a state of unrelenting misery. This is, of course, unfortunate, even lamentable. Yet one frequently discovers a lack of sympathy for the troubled youth. This dearth of compassion is undoubtedly due to the teenager's insistence upon dealing with his lot in an unduly boisterous fashion. He is, quite simply, at an age where he can keep nothing to himself. No impulse too fleeting, no sentiment too raw, that the teenager does not feel compelled to share it with those around him.

This sort of behavior naturally tends to have an alienating effect. And while this is oftimes its major intent, one cannot help but respond with hearty ill will.

Therefore, in the interest of encouraging if not greater understanding, at least greater decorum, I have set down the following words of advice.

If in addition to being physically unattractive you find that you do not get along well with others, do not under any circumstances attempt to alleviate this situation by developing an interesting personality. An interesting personality is, in an adult, insufferable. In a teenager it is frequently punishable by law.

———

Wearing dark glasses at the breakfast table is socially acceptable only if you are legally blind or partaking of your morning meal out of doors during a total eclipse of the sun.

———

Should your political opinions be at extreme variance with those of your parents, keep in mind that while it is indeed your constitutional right to express these sentiments verbally, it is unseemly to do so with your mouth full—particularly when it is full of the oppressor's standing rib roast.

———

Think before you speak. Read before you think. This will give you something to think about that you didn't make up yourself—a wise move at any age, but most especially at seventeen, when you are in the greatest danger of coming to annoying conclusions.

———

Try to derive some comfort from the knowledge that if your guidance counselor were working up to *his* potential, he wouldn't still be in high school.

———

The teen years are fraught with any number of hazards, but none so perilous as that which manifests itself as a tendency to consider movies an important art form. If you are presently, or just about to be, of this opinion, perhaps I can spare you years of unbearable pretension by posing this question: If movies (or films, as you are probably now referring to them) were of such a high and serious nature, can you possibly entertain even the slightest notion that they would show them in a place that sold Orange Crush and Jujubes?

———

It is at this point in your life that you will be giving the greatest amount of time and attention to matters of sex. This is not only acceptable, but should, in fact, be encouraged, for this is the last time that sex will be genuinely exciting. The more farsighted among you may wish to cultivate supplementary interests in order that you might have something to do when you get older. I personally recommend the smoking of cigarettes—a habit with staying power.

———

While we're on the subject of cigarettes, do not forget that adolescence is also the last time that you can reasonably expect to be forgiven a taste for a brand that might by way of exotic shape, color or package excite comment.

———

The girl in your class who suggests that this year the Drama Club put on *The Bald Soprano* will be a thorn in people's sides all of her life.

———

Should you be a teenager blessed with uncommon good looks, document this state of affairs by the taking of photographs. It is the only way anyone will ever believe you in years to come.

———

Avoid the use of drugs whenever possible. For while they may, at this juncture, provide a pleasant diversion, they are, on the whole, not the sort of thing that will in later years (should you *have* later years) be of much use in the acquisition of richly rewarding tax shelters and beachfront property.

———

If you reside in a state where you attain your legal majority while still in your teens, pretend that you don't. There isn't an adult alive who would want to be contractually bound by a decision he came to at the age of nineteen.

———

Remember that as a teenager you are at the last stage in your life when you will be happy to hear that the phone is for you.

———

Stand firm in your refusal to remain conscious during algebra. In real life, I assure you, there is no such thing as algebra.

———

At Home
with Pope Ron

I t is a clear, crisp day, the sunlight glinting brilliantly off the spires of St. Peter's Basilica—the entire scene as impressive and monumental as ever—but I scarcely notice as I make my hurried way across the square, for I am late for my interview and as any good journalist knows, popes don't like to be kept waiting. I enter the Vatican breathlessly, take quick note of the really quite attractive Swiss Guard and make my way to the papal apartments, where I am to meet the man who has arranged this interview—the cardinal bishop closest to the pope.

"Hi," says a tall, rather lanky fellow whom I would place in his very early thirties, "I'm Jeff Cardinal Lucas, but call me Jeff." Jeff extends a friendly hand and I, not being a Catholic, am somewhat at a loss as to what to do. Just then I am rescued from what could easily have turned into an extremely embarrassing situation, by a husky masculine voice. "Jeff, Jeff, if that's the girl from the magazine, tell her I'll be with her in a minute. I'm just finishing up an encyclical."

True to his word, sixty seconds later I am confronted by a tall, somewhat shaggy-haired man with startlingly long eyelashes and a ready, even impish, grin. "Hi," he says in that hauntingly deep voice that I had heard only a minute before. "I'm the Supreme Pontiff, but call me Ron—everyone does."

And much to my surprise I do, and *easily*, for Pope Ron's genuine warmth is infectious. Soon we are sitting comfortably on a big, old, leather sofa chatting away as if we had known each other forever. Before too long, we are joined by Sue, the pope's delicate blond wife of the pre-Raphaelite curls and long, tapering fingers, and Dylan, Ron's boyish little son from his first marriage.

I check my tape recorder to make sure it's working and ask Ron if he would like to start by telling me a little about his personal life, what he does to relax—to escape from the pressures of holiness and infallibility.

"Well," says Ron, "I would first like to say that this is, after all, the new Church and things have really loosened up around here. I mean, I do try to adapt to others. To understand and consider points of view different from my own. To grow. To extend myself. To explore the various regions of thought. You know, I have kind of a motto that I found to be of tremendous use to me in this job. A motto that I think has done a lot to make the Church really relevant. In fact, Sue here liked it so much that she made me this." Ron divests himself of his robe and reveals a white cotton T-shirt emblazoned in red with the legend INFALLIBLE BUT NOT INFLEXIBLE. "Of course," continues the pontiff, "this is just the prototype. As soon as Sue is finished with the urn she's working on now—you know, of course, that she's really incredible with the potter's wheel—she's going to see about having them made up for the entire Sacred College of Cardinals.

"As for relaxation, well, one of the things I really like to do is work with my hands. I mean, it really humbles a man, even a pope, to have tactile contact with the raw materials of nature. See that scepter over there? It took me six months to carve it out of rosewood, but it was worth it because by making it myself I feel that it's really a part of me, really mine." At this, Sue smiles proudly and gives Ron's ring a playful little kiss. It is easy to see what a terribly *happy* couple they are.

"I do other things too, things around the palace. Sue and I do them together, and even Dylan helps, don't you, Dyl?" Ron asks paternally as he rumples his young son's hair. "I mean, when we first moved in here you wouldn't have believed it. Incredibly formal, incredibly elaborate, unbelievably uptight. And it's such a big place really that we've barely made a dent. But one thing we have done—finished just last week, as a matter of fact, I mean Sue and I together, of course—was that we took the walls of the Sistine Chapel down to the natural brick, and now it really looks great, really warm, really basic."

We sip a little mint tea, and watch with amusement as little Dylan tries on his father's miter. I join in the gentle laughter as the large headdress falls over his little face. "Now for my next question, Ron, and I know you'll answer me honestly, I mean that goes without saying. Is the pope Catholic?"

"Look," he says, "if you mean me specifically, I mean me *personally,* yes, I am Catholic. But you know, of course, that this old bugaboo is no longer really applicable. The field is definitely opening up, and being Catholic really didn't swing my election as pope. The Sacred College of Cardinals looks for someone open to God, someone at home with his or her own feelings, someone, you might say, who can communicate rather than just excommunicate—which is, after all, so negative, so the opposite of the type of actualization that I hope the Church now represents. Yes, the Church is opening up to every possibility, and I see no reason why we can't expect in the not-too-distant future a Pope Rochester, a Pope Ellen, even a Pope Ira."

"Pope Ira?" I ask. "Isn't that a bit unlikely? A Jewish pope after the long Church history of saying that the Jews killed Christ?"

"Look," Ron pontificates, "what's past is past. You know we no longer blame the death of Christ on the Jews. I mean, obviously they were involved, but you have to look at things historically and nowadays the Church accepts the bull that I issued last year which decreed an acceptance of the fact that all they probably did was just hassle him, and that's what my bull decreed; the Jews *hassled* Christ, they didn't actually kill him."

Much relieved, I ask Ron about the early years, the struggle years, the tough years that every young man with scepters in his eyes must endure—nay, triumph over—if he is to reach his lordly goal.

"Yeah," says Ron, "it was rough, real rough, but it was fun too. I mean, I've done the whole thing, really gone the distance, from altar boy to the Big P. I've been there in the confessional listening to the little boys tell of impure thoughts. I've been there baptizing the babies—upfront so to speak." He chuckles softly at his own joke. "I've run the bingo games, married the faithful, tended the flock. I was the youngest cardinal ever to come out of the Five Towns, and it wasn't always easy, but I've had some laughs along the way and it was all worthwhile the night they elected me pope. I remember that night. It was warm and breezy and Pam and I—Pam was my first wife—stood together watching the smoke, waiting and waiting. Nine times, but it seemed like a million, until the smoke was white and I heard I'd made it. Jesus, it was beautiful, really beautiful."

Ron brushes away the tears that sentiment has evoked, but he is obviously unashamed of real emotion, free from the repression that has so long constrained men. I mention this and Ron is pleased, even grateful, that I have noticed his supremacy over the old, uptight values that deny men the right to their feelings.

"Look," he says dogmatically, and it is easy to see that the papacy has not been wasted on this man, "we're all in this together, you know—I mean, Sue and I are *partners.* We discuss everything, and I mean everything. I wouldn't consider issuing an edict without discussing it with her first. Not because she's my wife, but because I respect her opinion; I value her judgment. Lots of things she does on her own, like instituting the whole-grain host. I mean, that was *totally* her thing. It was *she* who pointed out to *me* that for years the faithful had been poisoning their systems with overly refined hosts. And that was only *one* of the things she's done. There are hundreds—I couldn't possibly name them all. Yeah, Sue is really something else. I mean, she has definitely got the interests of the faithful at heart. You've got to believe me when I say she's thinking of others all the time. She's not just my lady, man; she's *our* lady. And you can take it from me that that's no bull, that's strictly from the heart."

The Modern-Day
Lives of the Saints

S T. GARRETT THE PETULANT (died 1974): Patron of make-up artists, invoked against puffiness and uneven skin tone.

Garrett was born in Cleveland in 1955, or so he claimed. His father was a factory worker who took little interest in his pale, delicate son. His mother, a pious woman who supplemented the family income by selling cosmetics door-to-door, was perhaps Garrett's earthly inspiration.

From the time he was a very small child Garrett exhibited an almost precocious generosity of spirit, and was constantly volunteering to do "at least the eyes" of those females with whom he came in contact. At the age of eleven, clad only in rayon, he walked forty-seven miles in a terrible blizzard in order to place in the deepest forest an offering of food for the woodland creatures. The site of this blessed action is now often visited by pilgrims from all over the world, and is known as Cherries in the Snow. It was also around this time that Garrett performed his first miracle by correcting the appearance of a local matron's broad and fleshy nose without the visible use of contouring powder.

In the summer of his sixteenth year Garrett met a visiting New York stage actor in the Greyhound bus station, and it was through the kind offices of this man (whose own deep sense of humility has led him to request anonymity) that Garrett had his first great revlonation. Spent and trembling, he saw before him a large reflective surface surrounded by shining lights. He saw needful, begging eyes. He saw undefined cheekbones. He saw dry, parched lips. He saw an array of splendid colors. He saw his destiny.

Much inspired by Garrett's way, the actor assisted him in his journey to the city of New York. Here Garrett performed his second miracle by purchasing and furnishing a lavish co-op apartment despite the fact that he had no visible means of support.

News quickly spread throughout the city that Garrett was capable of truly amazing transformations. Women who were the recipients of his attentions called him Blessed and he was soon Venerated by all those in the know.

Despite his exalted position Garrett practiced humility and was often to be seen in rough districts of the city behaving in a most submissive manner while performing low and menial services for others. Garrett was found martyred in the bedroom of his East Side penthouse apartment late one Sunday morning.

ST. AMANDA OF NEW YORK, SOUTHAMPTON AND PALM BEACH (died 1971; came out 1951): Patroness of the well-bred, is invoked against the "cut direct," having to dip into capital and improper use of the word "home."

The daughter of Mr. and Mrs. Morgan Hayes Birmingham IV of New York, Southampton and Palm Beach, Amanda was born at Doctors Hospital in New York on January 3, 1933. She made her debut at the Gotham Ball and was a graduate of The Convent of the Sacred Heart and Manhattanville College. Her paternal grandfather, Morgan Hayes Birmingham III, was a member of the New York Stock Exchange and the founder of the firm of Birmingham, Stevens and Ryan. She was a descendant of Colonel Thomas M. Hayes.

Almost from birth it was apparent that Amanda was blessed with an almost sublime sense of tact. During her baptism at St. Ignatius Loyola she was the very picture of infant dignity and neither cried nor wriggled, despite the fact that the attending priest was generally thought to be something of an arriviste. Her childhood was characterized by a nearly fanatical attention to detail, and notice was first taken of her miraculous powers when at the age of three there appeared, appropriately placed about the nursery, Lalique vases filled with perfectly arranged, out-of-season flowers. The second indication of these powers occurred when Amanda, a mere nine years old, managed to correct, while dutifully attending her French class in New York, an extraordinarily indelicate seating plan committed by her maternal grandmother's social secretary in Hobe Sound.

Amanda's martyrdom took place during a weekend house party when she knowingly allowed herself to be served, *from the right,* a salad containing wild mushrooms picked by her host, rather than strike an unpleasant note by refusing.

ST. WAYNE (died circa 1975): Patron of middle children, invoked against whatever's left over.

Wayne was born two years after his brilliant and handsome brother Mike and three and a half years before his perfectly adorable sister Jane. Very little is remembered of his life and works, if any, and his canonization is the result of a unique mix-up in which Mike was made a saint twice and with typical generosity gave Wayne his extra sainthood.

ST. INGMAR-FRANÇOIS-JEAN-JONAS-ANDREW: Patron of graduate film students, invoked against going to the movies for fun, detractors of Stan Brakhage and disbelievers in the genius of John Ford.

St. Ingmar-François-Jean-Jonas-Andrew was born in a starkly lit delivery room in the kind of small American town that is all small American towns. From infancy he was astonishingly perceptive, and invariably saw layers of meaning not apparent to the average moviegoer. As early as his sixth birthday Ingmar-François-Jean-Jonas-Andrew displayed the remarkable dual tendency to overwrite and underexplain.

Among the many miracles to his credit are getting adults to actually attend a Jerry Lewis Film Festival and introducing a course at an accredited university entitled "The Philosophy of Busby Berkeley and Its Influence on Rainer Werner Fassbinder and Robert Bresson."

Rather than martyr himself, St. Ingmar-François-Jean-Jonas-Andrew sent one of his students.

The Servant Problem

I
t was just a few years ago that, owing to some rather
favorable publicity, I came into what is known as a little
money. This unexpected but most welcome piece of good
fortune enabled me for the very first time to secure living
quarters that one could, if pressed, describe as commodious.
I promptly set out to fix the place up, and soon acquired
some dandy home furnishings carefully chosen to give a false
impression of both my breeding and my background. Surrounded by these venerable objects, I cheerfully noted that
I had at long last achieved all three of my material goals: new
money, old furniture and a separate room to write in.

Due, however, to my unhappy penchant for whiling away
the hours (not to mention years) reading other people's
books, I was soon in possession of what looked very much
indeed like six small public libraries wherein smoking was
not merely allowed but actually, and even brutally, enforced.
Ashes to ashes, dust to dust. Were truer words ever spoken?
I think not. There was no question about it, I needed a maid,

and needed one badly. Unfortunately, I had not the slightest idea of how to go about getting one. This worried me enormously. I became flustered, then agitated, until finally I was compelled to take myself in hand and explain to myself calmly yet firmly that a maid was not, after all, the world's most exotic prize, and could undoubtedly be procured in a perfectly ordinary fashion. A couple of perfectly ordinary fashions came to mind but were shortly discounted. A store? No, it had been years since you could buy a maid, and even then, not in stores. A bar? Don't be ridiculous. I was looking for a maid, not an agent. Where then? I was, it seemed, stymied, stuck, stopped dead in my tracks, no place to go, nowhere to turn. Nowhere to turn, that is, until I fortuitously recalled a friend who had come into *her* money by accident of birth rather than by dint of hard work. Here was the very person to advise me, to smooth my path, to show me the way.

I quickly telephoned her and evidently displayed my ignorance to such great advantage that she agreed not only to help out but to actually get up a small group of likely candidates. She regretted, however, that since I was looking for someone to come only one day a week, I could not expect the sort of high-quality service that was routinely available on her own premises. I took this news admirably and awaited further instructions. A few days later she called to announce that she was sending over some possibilities for me to interview—and by interview, she stressed, she did not mean asking them where they got their ideas or if they had always been funny, but rather, where else they were employed, how much they charged and exactly what duties they were willing to perform. I was then to decide if I liked them—*as maids, not people.* She emphasized this not only as if the two were mutually exclusive but also in a tone of voice that I felt to be unduly withering. When I expressed these sentiments, she replied that she was merely cautioning me against imposing personal standards inappropriate to the situation. By this she apparently meant that you decided you liked a maid because she ironed, and not because she recognized you from being on the *Today* show. It was at this juncture that I began to suspect that having a maid might not be the fun it looked. Nevertheless, I persevered and agreed to begin the interviewing process immediately.

Later that same afternoon, the first applicant arrived in the form of an excessively well-groomed young man. Modern-day life, it seems, has given us not only girl ministers but also boy maids. I am in favor of neither, but seeing as how he was already standing there I let him in and politely offered to take his sweater. He declined, presumably because he didn't want to go to all the trouble of untying it. I attempted to lead him down the hall, but as we passed the bedroom something caught his eye and he wandered in to take a closer look. His attention had been captured by a small painting that hung over the fireplace.

"Decorative art," he stated. "I suppose you find it amusing."

"No," I replied, wondering how many times I had met this boy before, "I find it decorative."

"The bed?" he inquired with a lift of one eyebrow.

"Renaissance Revival," I parried—then thrust. "Attributed to Herter."

"Ah," he said, "American."

The interview, as far as I was concerned, was over. If he didn't dust American furniture there was little chance he did windows. Before, however, I could advise him of this, he had made his way into the living room, where I found him a moment later decoratively draped across my American sofa. He looked up as I entered, smiled graciously, and with an expressive little nod of his expressive little head, indicated that I might be seated. He then treated me to a lengthy monologue, the purpose of which was to acquaint me with his seriously rarefied sensibility. During the course of this, I tried several times to ask him how much he charged, having earlier hit upon the plan of hastening his leave-taking by offering him a highly minimum wage. But every time I raised the subject he deflected it. Obviously, he considered any discussion of money to be vulgar, tasteless and shockingly parvenu. Finally he stooped to breathe, and I inquired softly if perhaps rather than being paid he wouldn't just prefer that I quietly make a contribution to his favorite charity. This, so to speak, did the trick, and he left with no further fanfare.

Victory was mine to savor but briefly, for I had yet before me a seemingly endless procession of aspiring domestics. So unanimous were they in their two most untenable demands that with fair rapidity they became one big blur. Without exception, they insisted on coming to work during the day, and furthermore made it clear that they had every intention of coming to the house. I was loath, of course, to meet these stipulations, since during the day I am home not writing. During the night I am *out* not writing, and this, obviously, was the most convenient arrangement. I was, however, singularly unsuccessful in persuading any of them of this, and was eventually forced to choose the best of a bad and deplorably illogical lot. Ever mindful of my friend's advice, I picked the one that I liked best as a maid, and while the fact that she ironed most assuredly contributed to my feelings of affection, the fact that she spoke not a single word of English is, I must confess, what clinched the deal. If I was going to have to spend the entire day in the company of another, I most certainly preferred another who had not even the vaguest notion of what I was saying on the telephone.

The first few times she came we coexisted peacefully, if not lovingly, but by the fourth week I began to find the situation intolerable. Although I made every effort to stay out of her way, she was forever following me from room to room brandishing dangerous-looking household appliances and looking at me contemptuously in Portuguese. It was all too apparent that she had very little use for a person who, it seemed, spent all day long lying around the house using up towels and talking on the telephone in a foreign language. After one episode involving a particularly vigorous and disdainful emptying of ashtrays, I accepted the fact that henceforth I would be obliged to spend my day out of doors.

At first, going out during the day was kind of interesting. A lot of places were open, and it was undeniably well lit, though rather crowded and a tad noisy. I did my level best to if not enjoy, then at least to adapt myself. Soon, however, the novelty wore off, and I found it increasingly difficult to pursue my normal way of life in this alien and hostile environment. I was repeatedly harassed and ofttimes insulted by surly doormen who did not smile upon me fondly as I lolled about beneath their canopies, minding my own business and doing the *TV Guide* crossword puzzle. Crowds gathered and trouble brewed as I attempted to keep in touch with a wide circle of friends via public phone. And time after time

I was the innocent recipient of pointed remarks as I caught up on my reading while attractively posed atop the hoods of other people's parked cars.

Clearly, this could not go on forever; something had to be done, and fast. There were, of course, no easy answers. The problem was a serious one and demanded a serious effort if it was ever to be solved. To this end I was fully prepared to use every possible method at my disposal. Unfortunately, however, the possible methods at my disposal are rarely those involving careful research and painstaking detail. They tend, it is true, more in the direction of harebrained schemes and crackpot theories. In view of this, it is understandable that I was, in the end, unable to come to any firm resolution and can offer only the tangible written proof that I tried.

THE TANGIBLE WRITTEN PROOF THAT I TRIED

It was apparent to me that an apartment, like a sweater, was impossible to clean if one was in it. Following this logic, it was then equally apparent that an apartment, like a sweater, should be sent out to be cleaned. I decided that this could be accomplished by the general establishment of stores for this purpose. So far, so good. The kinks in this thing didn't show up until I came to the part where one went to pick up the apartment. It was at this point that I remembered the dirty-sweater analogy, and my heart sank. This sensation was simultaneously accompanied by a vision of myself standing at a counter screaming, "This is not my apartment! Don't you think I know what my own apartment looks like? Mine was the one with the separate room to write in and the two wood-burning fireplaces. This apartment is not mine. This apartment has no separate room to write in, only one wood-burning fireplace and a loft bed. Believe me, I don't have a loft bed. That I promise you. So don't tell me that this is my apartment, it's just that the rest of it didn't come back yet. And do you mind telling me how you could lose a wood-burning fireplace? *It was not hanging by a thread.* It was attached to a very substantial plaster wall. This isn't my apartment and I'm not taking it. No, I wouldn't rather have this apartment than no apartment at all. I want *my* apartment, the one I brought you. All right, I will—I *will* sue you. Don't think I won't. You'll hear from my lawyer. I'm going to call him right now."

And with that I saw myself turning on my heel and angrily stalking out. Lamentably, the next thing I saw was myself back outside, in a public phone booth with crowds gathering and trouble brewing. It was then that I decided that if I was going to have to make my phone calls outside anyway, I might as well keep both fireplaces.

Things

Things

All of the things in the world can be divided into two basic categories: natural things and artificial things. Or, as they are more familiarly known, nature and art. Now, nature, as I am only too well aware, has her enthusiasts, but on the whole, I am not to be counted among them. To put it rather bluntly, I am not the type who wants to go back to the land—I am the type who wants to go back to the hotel. This state of affairs is at least partially due to the fact that nature and I have so little in common. We don't go to the same restaurants, laugh at the same jokes or, most significant, see the same people.

This was not, however, always the case. As a child I was frequently to be found in a natural setting: playing in the snow, walking in the woods, wading in the pond. All these things were standard events in my daily life. But little by little I grew up, and it was during this process of maturation that I began to notice some of nature's more glaring deficiencies. First of all, nature is by and large to be found out of doors, a location where, it cannot be argued, there are never enough comfortable chairs. Secondly, for fully half of the time it is day out there, a situation created by just the sort of harsh overhead lighting that is so unflattering to the heavy smoker. Lastly, and most pertinent to this discourse, is the fact that natural things are by their very definition wild, unkempt and more often than not crawling with bugs. Quite obviously, then, natural things are just the kind of things that one does not strive to acquire. *Objets d'art* are one thing; *objets d'nature* are not. Who, after all, could possibly want to own something that even the French don't have a word for?

In view of all this I have prepared a little chart designed to more graphically illustrate the vast superiority of that which is manufactured over that which is not.

NATURE	*ART*
The sun	The toaster oven
Your own two feet	Your own two Bentleys
Windfall apples	Windfall profits
Roots and berries	Linguini with clam sauce
Time marching on	The seven-second delay
Milk	Butter
The good earth	25 percent of the gross
Wheat	Linguini with clam sauce
A man for all seasons	Marc Bohan for Dior
Ice	Ice cubes
Facial hair	Razor blades
The smell of the countryside after a long, soaking rain	Linguini with clam sauce
TB	TV
The mills of God	Roulette
A tinkling mountain brook	Paris

Now that you have had an opportunity to gain an overview of the subject, it is time to explore things more thoroughly, time to ask yourselves what you have learned and how you can best apply your new-found knowledge. Well, obviously, the first and most important thing you have learned is that linguini with clam sauce is mankind's crowning achievement. But as this is a concept readily grasped, it is unnecessary to linger over it or discuss it in greater detail.

As to the question of how you can best apply what you have learned, I believe that it would be highly beneficial to you all were we to examine the conventional wisdom on the subject of things in order to see what it looks like in the light of your new-found knowledge:

THE CONVENTIONAL WISDOM ON THE SUBJECT OF THINGS AS SEEN IN THE LIGHT OF YOUR NEW-FOUND KNOWLEDGE

All good things come to those who wait: This is a concept that parallels in many respects another well-known thought, that of the meek inheriting the earth. With that in mind, let us use a time-honored method of education and break the first statement into its two major component parts: a) All good things; b) come to those who wait. Immediately it is apparent that thanks to our previous study we are well informed as to which exactly the good things are. It is when we come to "those who wait" that we are entering virgin territory. Educators have found that in cases like this it is often best to use examples from actual life. So then, we must think of a place that from our own experience we know as a place where "those who wait" might, in fact, be waiting.

Thus I feel that the baggage claim area of a large metropolitan airport might well serve our purpose.

Now, in addressing the fundamental issue implied by this question—i.e., the veracity of the statement "All good things come to those who wait"—we are in actuality asking the question, "Do, in fact, all good things come to those who wait?" In breaking our answer into *its* two major component parts, we find that we know that: a) among "all good things" are to be found linguini with clam sauce, the Bentley automobile and the ever-fascinating city of Paris.

We also know that: b) "those who wait" are waiting at O'Hare. We then think back to our own real-life adventures, make one final check of our helpful chart and are sadly compelled to conclude that "No, all good things do *not* come to those who wait"—unless due to unforeseeably personal preferences on the part of "those who wait," "all good things" are discovered to include an item entitled SOME OF YOUR LUGGAGE MISSING ALL OF ITS CONTENTS.

A thing of beauty is a joy forever: This graceful line from a poem written by John Keats is not so much inaccurate as it is archaic. Mr. Keats, it must be remembered, was not only a poet but also a product of the era in which he lived. Additionally, it must not be forgotten that one of the salient features of the early nineteenth century was an inordinate admiration for the simple ability to endure. Therefore, while a thing of beauty is a joy, to be sure, we of the modern age, confined no longer by outmoded values, are free to acknowledge that nine times out of ten a weekend is long enough.

Each man kills the thing he loves: And understandably so, when he has been led to believe that it will be a joy forever.

Doing your own thing: the use of the word "thing" in this context is unusually precise, since those who are prone to this expression actually do *do* things as opposed to those who do work—i.e., pottery is a thing—writing is a work.

Life is just one damned thing after another: And death is a cabaret.

Pointers for Pets

I feel compelled by duty to begin this discourse with what I actually think of as a statement, but what will more probably be construed as an admission. I do not like animals. Of any sort. I don't even like the idea of animals. Animals are no friends of mine. They are not welcome in my house. They occupy no space in my heart. Animals are off my list. I will say, however, in the spirit of qualification, that I mean them no particular harm. I won't bother animals if animals won't bother me. Well, perhaps I had better amend that last sentence. I won't *personally* bother animals. I do feel, though, that a plate bereft of a good cut of something rare is an affront to the serious diner, and that while I have frequently run across the fellow who could, indeed, be described as a broccoli-and-potatoes man, I cannot say that I have ever really taken to such a person.

Therefore, I might more accurately state that I do not like animals, with two exceptions. The first being in the past tense, at which point I like them just fine, in the form of nice crispy spareribs and Bass Weejun penny loafers. And the second being outside, by which I mean not merely outside, as in outside the house, but genuinely outside, as in outside in the woods, or preferably outside in the South American jungle. This is, after all, only fair. I don't go there; why should they come here?

The above being the case, it should then come as no surprise that I do not approve of the practice of keeping animals as pets. "Not approve" is too mild: pets should be disallowed by law. Especially dogs. Especially in New York City.

I have not infrequently verbalized this sentiment in what now passes for polite society, and have invariably been the recipient of the information that even if dogs should be withheld from the frivolous, there would still be the blind and the pathologically lonely to think of. I am not totally devoid of compassion, and after much thought I believe that I have hit upon the perfect solution to this problem—let the lonely lead the blind. The implementation of this plan would provide companionship to one and a sense of direction to the other, without inflicting on the rest of the populace the all too common spectacle of grown men addressing German shepherds in the respectful tones best reserved for elderly clergymen and Internal Revenue agents.

You animal lovers uninterested in helping news dealers across busy intersections will just have to seek companionship elsewhere. If actual friends are not within your grasp, may I suggest that you take a cue from your favorite celebrity and consider investing in a really good entourage. The advantages of such a scheme are inestimable: an entourage is indisputably superior to a dog (or even, of course, actual friends), and will begin to pay for itself almost immediately. You do not have to walk an entourage; on the contrary, one of the major functions of an entourage is that *it* walks *you.*

You do not have to name an entourage. You do not have to play with an entourage. You do not have to take an entourage to the vet—although the conscientious entourage owner makes certain that his entourage has had all of its shots. You do, of course, have to feed an entourage, but this can be accomplished in decent Italian restaurants and without the bother and mess of large tin cans and special plastic dishes.

If the entourage suggestion does not appeal to you, perhaps you should alter your concept of companionship. Living things need not enter into it at all. Georgian silver and Duncan Phyfe sofas make wonderful companions, as do all alcoholic beverages and out-of-season fruits. Use your imagination, study up on the subject. You'll think of something.

If, however, you do not think of something—and animal lovers being a singularly intractable lot, chances are that you won't—I have decided to direct the remainder of my remarks to the pets themselves in the hope that they might at least learn to disport themselves with dignity and grace.

If you are a dog and your owner suggests that you wear a sweater . . . suggest that he wear a tail.

———

If you have been named after a human being of artistic note, run away from home. It is unthinkable that even an animal should be obliged to share quarters with anyone who calls a cat Ford Madox Ford.

———

Dogs who earn their living by appearing in television commercials in which they constantly and aggressively demand meat should remember that in at least one Far Eastern country they *are* meat.

———

If you are only a bird in a gilded cage—count your blessings.

———

A dog who thinks he is man's best friend is a dog who obviously has never met a tax lawyer.

———

If you are an owl being kept as a pet, I applaud and encourage your tendency to hoot. You are to be highly commended for expressing such a sentiment. An owl is, of course, not a pet at all; it is an unforgivable and wistful effort in the direction of whimsy.

———

No animal should ever jump up on the dining-room furniture unless absolutely certain that he can hold his own in the conversation.

———

The Frances Ann
Lebowitz Collection

F ollowing are a few selected pages from the forthcoming auction catalogue of the estate of Frances
Ann Lebowitz.

Length 19 inches (48 cm)

See illustration.

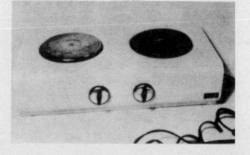

1. KORD (BRAND NAME)

Thus is inscribed this important example of popularly priced
hot plate. White enameled metal with black brand-name
inscription and dials, this two-burner plate was personally

delivered to its present owner by Mr. Roper, the absentee building superintendent long thought to be a mythical figure. While actual physical manifestation of Mr. Roper is of keen interest to those scholars and collectors dedicated to a more detailed and esoteric study of *Memento Pori,* or *Reminders of Poverty,* it should be noted that his appearance was a singular one and that he himself is not offered with this lot.

The Kord, however, replaced an earlier hot plate widely believed to have been formerly owned (and used) by all of Mr. Roper's antecedents.

The Kord is interestingly proportioned, featuring two burners but lacking room for two pans. This feature possibly derives from the landlord's insistence on thematic discomfort.

The Frances Ann Lebowitz Collection, one of the largest ever assembled (in an apartment of that size) of *Memento Pori* effectively chronicles man's reaction to having no money from the end of the nineteen-sixties, through latter-nineteen-seventies acquisitions, until the present day.

All artistic media are represented: carvings in furniture, impressions in wall paint, and works in many metal alloys.

To explore all the various moods and historic events that influenced the creation of these objects would be a lengthy task. Some are flimsy, some jerry-built and others merely outmoded, but all seem to reflect man's underpayment of writers on this earth.

The Kord hot plate with its two burners and two dials reminds us that lack of funds is the ultimate poverty and that there is no way to avoid this fact. Possibly the inscription under each dial states it most clearly: *High, Medium, Low.*

2. BROIL KING TOASTER OVEN
   EARLY/LATE NINETEEN-SIXTIES

Emblazoned on one side with the Broil King logo, a sort of crown, and on the other side with the legend "infra red Bake 'N' Broil." Trimmed in black plastic, containing aluminum rack and glasslike window, ornamental wire and plug.

Length 17 inches (43 cm)

See illustration.

3. IMPORTANT ROWE SLEEP-OR-SOFA SOFA BED
SECOND HALF NINETEEN SEVENTY-ONE

Executed in plywood, upholstered with a foam-type substance and covered in brown wide-wale cotton corduroy; mattress in blue, gray and white ticking, black-and-white clothish label (do not remove under penalty of law).

Width: 3 feet (.9 m) (when sofa)
6 feet (1.8 m) (when bed)

See illustration.

4. PRIM ROSE CHINA HAND-PAINTED UNDER GLAZE
   BY NATIONAL BROTHERHOOD OF OPERATIVE POTTERS
   NINETEEN THIRTY-NINE?

Once the everyday dairy dishes of Mr. and Mrs. Phillip Splaver of Derby, Connecticut, these dessert and dinner plates were originally acquired at the West End Movie Theater in Bridgeport, Connecticut. Fortuitously (the theater owner was Mr. Splaver's brother-in-law), these outstanding vessels (once part of a complete set) painted with gray, black and red streaks on a field of white, were obtained without the principals being compelled to attend a wearying succession of Dish Nights. *3 pieces.*

Diameters: 10 1/2 inches (26.6 cm)
7 1/2 inches (19 cm)

See illustration.

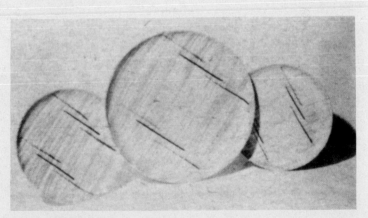

5. GROUP OF SMALL BOXES
MID-NINETEEN-SEVENTY-EIGHT

The first a red, white and blue cardboard Ambassador tooth-pick box containing many of the original 250 round tooth-picks; two cardboard Gem paper-clip boxes in outstanding shades of green; and a four-color (one an important translu-cent flesh tone) metal box stating contents of three sizes of Johnson & Johnson Band-Aid brand plastic strips. Interest-ing packaging error (lacking juniors). *4 pieces.*

Lengths: 2 3/4 to 3 1/4 inches
(7 to 8.2 cm)

6. THREE ELECTRICAL ALARM CLOCKS,
ONE OF WHICH WORKS
LATISH-TWENTIETH-CENTURY

The first two by Westclox (La Salle, Ill.), both lacking "crys-tals" but of interesting design: one almost starkly una-dorned, the other featuring horizontally striped border in tones of tangerine and black. The third a functional time-piece with numerals depicted in a pseudo-iridescent green that very nearly approach trompe l'oeil in that they give every impression of being visible in the dark; amusingly brand-named Lux. *3 pieces.*

Lengths: 3 3/4 to 4 1/4 inches
(9.5 to 11 cm)

See illustration.

7. TYPEWRITER
TWENTIETH-CENTURY

Remington Rand, gray metal, eleven stuck keys, unwound ribbon; the whole, a mess.

Length 11 inches (28 cm)

See illustration.

8. ANOTHER TYPEWRITER
TWENTIETH-CENTURY

On loan from generally anonymous art director, lettera DL, two-toned gray metal; neither lot number 7 nor lot number 8 ever used by present owner.

Length 10 inches (25.4 cm)

9. COLLECTION OF FIVE EGGS
NOT QUITE AS LATE-TWENTIETH-CENTURY
AS ONE WOULD HAVE HOPED

Representing eggs in two modes, hard-boiled and raw: three of former, two of latter. Together with medium-blue cardboard egg carton and enamel saucepan similarly colored. *5 pieces* (at the moment).

10. PAIR OF INDUSTRIAL QUALITY EARPLUGS
EARLY-MORNING

Pair of vivid-yellow foam earplugs, to no avail. *2 pieces.*

Lengths 1 inch (2.54 cm)

11. TWO TAN OBJECTS
TWENTIETH-CENTURY

One a pepper mill and the other a salad bowl. Both somewhat the worse for wear. *2 pieces*

Height: 3 3/8 inches (8.16 cm)
Diameter: 6 inches (15 cm)

See illustration.

Drawings and Sculpture

12. ANONYMOUS
   BODY OF ALLIGATOR ON
   ASHTRAY BASE

Unsigned.
Ceramic, brown, yellow, blue and white.
Inscribed FLORIDA.

Height: 21 1/2 inches (54.5 cm)

See illustration.

13. FRAN LEBOWITZ
   A NUMBER OF DOODLES

Signed and dated '78.
Ballpoint pen under pressure.

*5 × 3 inches
(12.7 × 7.6 cm)*

14. FRIEND'S CHILD
    "GOOD MORNING, MOM!"

Illegibly signed.
Crayon on coloring book.

11 × 7 3/4 inches
(28 × 20 cm)

See illustration.

"Good Morning, Mom!"

15. EDITOR
  DON'T WRITE TILL YOU GET WORK

Unsigned and rather dated.
Colored pencil on purloined office stationery.

8 1/2 × 5 1/2 inches
(21.5 × 14 cm)

See illustration.

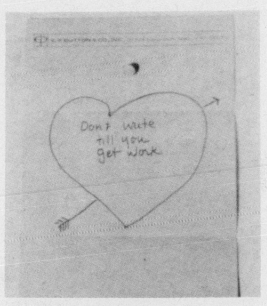

16. RUGS

TWO RECENTLY LAUNDERED
COTTON TERRY BATHMATS
LATE NINETEEN-SIXTIES

The first rather mauve in color, the second an unusually common shade of blue; both nice. *2 pieces.*

Approx. 3 feet (.9 m) × 1 foot 8 inches (50.8 cm)

See illustration.

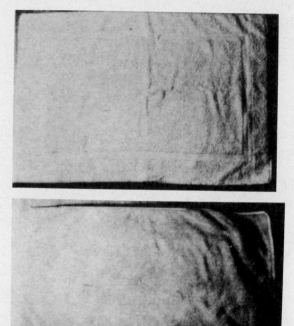

The Pen of My Aunt
Is on the Operating Table

A furnished apartment? No, I don't think so. I'm really not interested in a furnished apartment. No, really. Not at all. Not a furnished apartment. High tech? Yes, I know about high tech. Yes, I do. Really, I do. I know all about high tech.

I know about Sloan-Kettering too, but that doesn't mean that I feel like going up there and taking a look around.

No. Absolutely. No. Which building? Really? Oh, I love that building. That's a terrific building. I didn't know that you handled that building. You have an exclusive? Well. Aren't there any unfurnished apartments in that building? Oh. Yes, of course, the market. I know. I see. Yes, that's true, something else might come up there. Well, all right, but I'm really not interested in a furnished apartment. Not at all.

I can't believe this. I can't believe I'm going up there. A furnished apartment. I don't want a furnished apartment. A furnished apartment is out of the question. I hate furnished apartments. Although I can't imagine describing anything even remotely related to high tech as furnished. Equipped would be a better word, or maybe engineered. Every time I see one of those places I'm tempted to ask how many miles it gets to the gallon. Or where the boiler room is. Or the intensive care unit. The last time I was in a place like that I spent the better part of an hour skulking around looking for a brass plate inscribed with the name of the donor. High tech. I can't believe it.

Oh, hello. Yes, nice to see you again too. Sure, let's go right up.

Well, well, isn't this something. Oh, listen, I'm sorry but I don't seem to have a token with me. Do you think I could possibly borrow one from you? What? No turnstile? Yes, just an oversight, I'm sure. Some people just have no eye for detail. Then again, he may merely have been exercising his artistic restraint. He probably thought that the urinals in the living room were enough. A nice touch. Functional too, particularly for someone of his tastes—I mean taste. Well, now there's something I never would have thought of—a neon basketball hoop for a night light—it absolutely never would have occurred to me. It's quite an idea, though. Very thought-provoking. Visual humor. I've always loved visual humor. I wonder if I know anyone who knows Julius Erving? Probably not. Too bad, he might be interested in this. You know what they say about turnabout being fair play. Maybe at the next

*Philadelphia game he could shoot the ball into a night light.
He'd probably get a kick out of that. I know I certainly would.*

*Hmmmm, lookee there, will you. I mean, take a gander at
that. A genuine scrub sink with built-in instrument trays.*

No, no, I didn't notice that.

*A knee-controlled faucet too. Isn't that handy. Must be
just the thing for washing your hands when they're full. Yes,
it certainly does go beautifully with the chrome-plated hand
rails and hospital bathtub. All in all, I guess you'd have to
say that this is the bathroom that has everything. If you can't
get it here, you can't get it period. Scrub up, towel off and just
enough time for a little brain scan before bed. Nothing elaborate, just something to put your mind at ease and help you
sleep.*

The dining room? Of course, I'd love to see the dining
room.

*Look, let's be honest here. I'd love to see anything now.
Who knows how much time I have left? Anyway, maybe the
dining room will cheer me up. Maybe the dining room will
cheer me up? Who am I kidding? After that bathroom, open-
heart surgery would cheer me up. A weekend in Teheran with
the Ayatollah Khomeini would be a breath of fresh air. A visit
from the IRS would be like the month of May. Cheer me up?
I'll tell you what would cheer me up. It would cheer me up
if, in retaliation, the Ford Motor Company redecorated every
one of their plants in rose velvet love seats, fringed throw
pillows and teak cigarette tables. It would cheer me up if I
could sneak back in here tonight and pin a few doilies
around. It would cheer me up if tomorrow morning Congress
voted by an overwhelming majority to make the possession of
stainless-steel furniture a federal offense. It would cheer me*

up if only somehow I could arrange for my grandmother to get her hands on this place. Or Sister Parrish. Or my grandmother and Sister Parrish.

Yes. Absolutely. A spectacular hallway.

A spectacular hallway? Listen, this would be a spectacular runway. I can see it now. A DC-10 coming in for a landing, refracted light glinting off the glass brick, right through here. Perfect. Masterful. The takeoff might be a problem, but what the hell, if it has to stay, it has to stay. There's simply no such thing as too much storage space.

Ah, the dining room. The dining room. Pretty impressive. No amphitheater, of course, but this place has probably been cut up. Undoubtedly the amphitheater is in the next apartment. Just my luck: no working amphitheater. Oh, well, this sure is a clean dining room. Nice long table too. Shiny, real shiny. And rugged. A nice mix. Must be interesting eating here. First a small but tasteful dish of number ten nails and then on to the Salk vaccine. I wonder what kind of wine you serve with the Salk vaccine. I wonder what you serve the wine in. You probably just inject it. I wonder where the syringe goes. On the left or on the right? What if it's a formal dinner and you're serving more than one wine? And what about the help? What if they're clumsy and a guest begins to bleed profusely? All over the rubber floor. Does blood come off rubber? I wonder if Pirelli makes actual dinner guests. Good, substantial, economically designed, pared-down dinner guests. Yes, rubber dinner guests, that's the ticket.

Big room. Very spacious. Maybe too spacious. Out of scale. If I owned this place I think I'd install two x-ray technicians a little off center at either end of the room. Fairly short x-ray technicians, about 5'5", 5'6", nothing taller. Bring the proportions down a little, make it more livable. And maybe, just to amuse the eye, a single black orderly set catty-corner right over there. Just one. On an angle. Yes.

The kitchen? Well, I'm not much of a cook myself, but sure, I've come this far, let's see the kitchen.

This is definitely the kitchen, all right, no mistaking it. I guess the mess hall must be back there. Lots of big stuff in here. Nothing namby-pamby about this kitchen. And talk about light, it's positively sunstruck. Couldn't possibly be depressed in this place. Not if you tried. No siree, no matter how many times you pulled K.P. you'd just have to smile. Nice counter, too. Pretty stools. What do they call this place, anyway—Joe's Co-op & Grill? Some kitchen. A lot of people could use a kitchen like this. Boys Town, for one. Nairobi. The International Ladies' Garment Workers' Union. AFTRA. Yes, indeed, a lot of people could use a kitchen like this. But somehow I'm afraid that I'm just not one of them. I mean, how would it look in that big glass-windowed refrigerator to see right on the shelf—yes, right over there, where the plasma should be—two grapefruits, an elderly piece of Swiss cheese and half a bottle of club soda? No, it just wouldn't look right.

The bedroom? Yes, the bedroom. No, I hadn't forgotten the bedroom.

Sleep? In here? Surely a joke. A cruel joke. Sleep, you say? For how long? Until when? What time is reveille around here, anyway? Five? Six?

Yes, I did. I did notice the bed. Seen one like it before? No, not really.

Not one that big, anyway. Certainly not that big. How could all the pieces fit in the box? Even the deluxe set.

No, I don't think I'll try it out, actually.

I've always been sort of squeamish. Silly, I guess, but I'm

*kind of afraid I'll cut myself. Nothing personal, mind you—
I mean I'm sure if you're careful, it's perfectly safe. Perfectly.*

Yes. Certainly. Go right ahead.

*In this place you probably need a dime. Maybe I can get
out of here before she's finished. I really don't know what to
say to her. Is she going to pressure me? Discuss financing? Do
you apply for a mortgage, or are you taken before a judge and
sentenced? She said something about low maintenance. I
wonder whether she meant that it was less than $750 a month
or that you could just hose the whole place down.*

*What if this sort of thing really catches on and people start
winning this stuff on game shows? Yes, that's right, Mrs.
Smith, twenty pounds of slotted-angle elements, and that's
not all—yes, Mrs. Smith, that's right, this beautiful three-
piece set of simple wire bicycle baskets too—all yours, Mrs.
Smith, and thank you for playing our game.*

*Oh no, here she comes. What will I say? I don't want to
insult her. After all, someday a* real *apartment might come
up in this building. I know. I'll tell her that I just can't afford
it, that it's out of my league, that it needs too much work. It's
a shame, though. I really do love the building. I wonder what
it would cost to take the cement walls down to the natural
mahogany paneling. No, out of the question. Just another
crazy dream.*

Places

Places

Perhaps one of the most notable features of contemporary life is the unprecedented expansion of the concept of freedom of thought. This has led to any number of unpleasant developments, but none more disconcerting than the fact that place, once that most fixed of entities, has now become a matter of personal opinion. This state of affairs has manifested itself in countless ways, and one can no longer take comfort and sustenance from knowing one's place, keeping one's place, taking one's place or finding one's place.

The list, of course, does not end here. I could and would go on and on, were there not a larger issue at stake. For the hazards set forth on this list, grave though they be, are relatively insignificant when measured against the knowledge that one's place of residence, traditionally a cold, hard fact, has now become subject to individual perception. Obviously, this is hardly a situation that can be allowed to continue. Therefore, at the risk of being labeled alarmist, I must state unequivocally that when one's own home, historically a representational art form, becomes vulnerable to what can only be called creeping conceptualism, it is high time that something be done.

Too late, you say? Time's run out? It's gone too far? I think not. There are still many of us left who, when asked where we live, reply with logic and conviction. New York, we say, or Boston. Philadelphia. Des Moines. We're a small group but a varied one, and I feel quite strongly that by hard work and perseverance we can vanquish forever those among us who, realizing instinctively that they could never win, decided instead to place.

The first step, of course, in any successful battle plan is to identify the enemy, and thus I have defined the following terms:

PEOPLE WHO THINK OF THEMSELVES AS INHABITANTS OF THE PLANET, OR EARTHMAN

Plainly given to gross generalization, Earthman is immediately recognizable by a relationship to green, leafy vegetables that can best be described as camaraderie. He eats and thinks low on the food chain and often believes in reincarnation—a theory that at least explains where he gets his money. His favorite book is something called *The Whole Earth Catalog,* from which he apparently orders his clothes, and he is so frequently to be seen gazing at the stars that one can only hope that he is thinking of moving.

PEOPLE WHO THINK OF THEMSELVES AS CITIZENS OF THE WORLD, OR INTERNATIONALMAN

Best typified by the big-time Italian fashion designer, Internationalman is at home wherever he goes. He knows all the best restaurants, all the best languages and is one of the few remaining people left alive to still carry cash—not to mention paintings. Although fun at parties, Internationalman has an effect that one is compelled to characterize as trivializing. What, after all, is London to a man who thinks of the whole Middle East as just another bad neighborhood and the coast of South Africa as simply the beach?

And how is it that with so much to do and see, Internationalman is still able to devote such huge amounts of time and attention to the driving up of co-op prices in the borough of Manhattan? An endeavor, I believe, which will eventually result in transforming the entire city of New York into a resort area comparable to Acapulco in the fifties. Here former native writers will be obliged to work in the kitchens of luxury hotels cutting grapefruits into fancy shapes for the pleasure of Internationalman—a customer who will not, by the way, probably be very much interested in meeting your virgin sister.

PEOPLE WHO LIVE TOO FAR DOWNTOWN, OR LOFTMAN

People who live in lofts shouldn't throw stones, especially when they are in the enviable position of being able to sell them. Although SoHo has probably sprung to your mind, I am not, I assure you, that parochial, and can, due to unfortunate personal experience, report that such neighborhoods are now to be found in practically every minor American city. Usually occupying a renovated waterfront area, the quiche district, as I am wont to call it, has brought new and unwelcome meaning to the words "light industry."

You are advised that Loftman, appearances to the contrary, is really a fellow traveler of Earthman, and thus to be avoided assiduously.

PEOPLE WHO LOOK LIKE THEY LIVE AT THE SEATTLE AIRPORT, OR SALESMAN

Salesman, as he is commonly known, is a pretty harried-looking guy. Wandering as he does from gate to gate, it is no wonder that ofttimes he doubts his own sanity. Constantly he hears voices issuing instructions to what are openly referred to as "arriving Northwest Airlines passengers." It sounds very official; it even sounds real. Salesman, however, is nobody's fool and is well aware of the fact that there is no such thing as an arriving Northwest Airlines passenger—that when it comes to a Northwest Airlines passenger there is only a departing. In fact, at any given airport at any given time fully three quarters of the airport population consists entirely of departing Northwest Airlines passengers.

It is only to be expected, then, that people who spend so much time together would come to think of themselves as a community, with all that implies. Thus they have formed their own short-lived romantic attachments, developed their own cuisine based on the indigenous smoked almond and are enviably free of social unrest, having already been assigned classes by the airline.

Yet despite all this, Salesman is unhappy, for he knows that although he is headed straight for the top, he's just kidding himself to think he will ever really arrive.

Lesson One

LOS ANGELES, *laws AN juh lus,* or *laws ANG guh lus,* Calif., is a large citylike area surrounding the Beverly Hills Hotel. It is easily accessible to New York by phone or plane (although the converse is not true).

In 1956 the population of Los Angeles was 2,243,901. By 1970 it had risen to 2,811,801, 1,650,917 of whom are currently up for a series.

Early Spanish settlers called Los Angeles El Pueblo de Nuestra Señora la Reina de los Angeles, which means The Town of Our Lady, Queen of the Angels. The first part of the name was dropped when Los Angeles became a Mexican city in 1835. Today Los Angeles is often called collect.

The Land and Its Resources

LOCATION, SIZE AND SURFACE FEATURES

Los Angeles lies on the Pacific Coast approximately three thousand miles from midtown Manhattan. The terrain is varied and ranges from clay to grass to composition, depending upon the type of court you find most comfortable. Los Angeles is on the large side, covering over four hundred and fifty square miles, which makes it advisable to play close to the net.

Surface features are numerous, and include hills, palm trees, large billboards depicting former and future back-up singers, highly colored flowers, eye-tucks, parking attendants and an enormous sign spelling out the word "Hollywood," the purpose of which is to indicate that one has indeed gotten off the plane.

CURRENCY

The most popular form of currency in Los Angeles is the point. Points are what they give to writers instead of money. Curiously enough, it is impossible to use points to purchase either goods or services, a situation that makes imperative the possession of a round-trip airplane ticket.

CLIMATE

It is generally quite sunny in Los Angeles, thereby allowing the natives to read contracts by natural light. The mild weather is one of the main topics of conversation in Los Angeles, the other one being the lack thereof in New York.

Many tourists come to Los Angeles because of the climate, attracted no doubt by the pleasant glare and festive air colors.

CHIEF PRODUCTS

The chief products of Los Angeles are novelizations, salad, game-show hosts, points, muscle tone, mini-series and re-writes. They export all of these items with the twin exceptions of muscle tone and points, neither of which seem to travel well.

The People

Many of the people in Los Angeles appear so lifelike that a sharp eye is necessary in order to avoid conversation with those who may be too dead to offer points. Initiates will carefully study a prospective producer's gold neckchain and will not start talking until certain that it is moving rhythmically.

The inhabitants of Los Angeles are a warm people, and family ties are so strong that a florist may volunteer the information that his sister-in-law's stepmother was once married to Lee Major's great-uncle before one has had a chance to ask.

EVERYDAY LIFE AND CUSTOMS

Everyday life in Los Angeles is casual but highly stratified and can probably best be understood by realizing that the residents would be happiest with a telephone book that contained subscribers' first names, followed by an announcement that the party had four lines, sixteen extensions and a fiercely guarded unlisted number.

FOOD AND DRINK

A great many people in Los Angeles are on special diets that restrict their intake of synthetic foods. The reason for this appears to be a widely held belief that organically grown fruits and vegetables make the cocaine work faster.

One popular native dish is called gambei and is served exclusively in Mr. Chow's, an attractive little Chinese restaurant on North Camden Drive. The menu description of gambei reads as follows: "This mysterious dish is everybody's favorite. People insist it is seaweed because it tastes and looks just like seaweed. But in fact it is not. It's a secret." This mystery was recently solved by a visiting New York writer, who took one taste of her surprise and said, "Grass."

"Grass?" queried her dinner companion. "You mean marijuana?"

"No," the writer replied. "Grass—you know, lawns, grass. The secret is that every afternoon all of the gardeners in Beverly Hills pull up around the back, the cook takes delivery and minutes later the happy patrons are avidly consuming—at $3.50 per portion—crisply French-fried—their own backyards."

CULTURE

Los Angeles is a contemporary city, and as such unfettered by the confining standards of conventional art. Therefore the people of this modern-day Athens have been free to develop new and innovative forms all their own. Of these, the most interesting is the novelization, for this enables one, for perhaps the very first time, to truly appreciate the phrase, "One picture is worth a thousand words."

DRESS

The garb of Los Angeles is colorful, with lemon yellow, sky blue and lime green predominating, particularly in the attire of middle-aged men, most of whom look like Alan King. It is customary for these men to leave unbuttoned the first five buttons of their shirts in a rakish display of gray chest hair. Visitors are warned that calling the police to come in and button everyone up is a futile gesture; they will not respond.

Teenagers of both sexes wear T-shirts that disprove the theory that the young are no longer interested in reading, and facial expressions that disprove the T-shirts.

Middle-aged women favor for daytime wear much the same apparel as do teenage girls, but after six they like to pretty up and generally lean toward prom clothes.

THE LANGUAGE

Alphabet and pronunciation were both borrowed from the English, as was the custom of reading receipts from left to right. Word usage is somewhat exotic, however, and visitors would do well to study carefully the following table of words and phrases:

Formal: long pants

Concept: car chase

Assistant Director: the person who tells the cars which way to go. The phrase for this in New York is traffic cop.

Director: the person who tells the assistant director which way to tell the cars to go. The phrase for this in New York is traffic cop.

Creative Control: no points

Take a Meeting: this phrase is used in place of "have a meeting," and most likely derives from the fact that "take" is the verb that the natives are most comfortable with.

Sarcasm: what they have in New York instead of Jacuzzis.

TRANSPORTATION

There are two modes of transport in Los Angeles: car and ambulance. Visitors who wish to remain inconspicuous are advised to choose the latter.

ARCHITECTURE

The architecture of Los Angeles is basically the product of a Spanish heritage and a rich inner life. Public buildings, which are called gas stations *(gaz TAY shuns)* or restaurants *(res tur ONTS),* are characterized by their lack of height and are generally no taller than your average William Morris agent, although they occasionally hold more people. Houses, which are called homes *(HOMZ),* can be distinguished from public buildings by the number of Mercedes-Benzes parked outside. If there are over twelve, it is fairly safe to assume that they take American Express.

Diary of
a New York
Apartment Hunter

Friday: Awakened at the crack of dawn by a messenger bearing this coming Sunday's *New York Times* Real Estate section. First six apartments gone already. Spent a good fifteen minutes dividing the number of *New York Times* editors into the probable number of people looking for two-bedroom apartments. Spent additional half-hour wondering how anyone who has a paper to get out every day could possibly have time to keep up eleven hundred friendships. Realized this theory not plausible and decided instead that the typesetters all live in co-ops with wood-burning fireplaces. Wondered briefly why listings always specify *wood-burning* fireplaces. Decided that considering the prices they're asking, it's probably just a warning device for those who might otherwise figure what the hell, and just burn money.

Called V.F. and inquired politely whether anyone in his

extremely desirable building had died during the night. Reply in the negative. I just don't get it. It's quite a large building and no one in it has died for months. In my tiny little building they're dropping like flies. Made a note to investigate the possibility that high ceilings and decorative moldings prolong life. Momentarily chilled by the thought that someone who lives in a worse building than mine is waiting for *me* to die. Cheered immeasurably by realization that a) nobody lives in a worse building than mine and b) particularly those who are waiting for me to die.

Saturday: Uptown to look at co-op in venerable midtown building. Met real estate broker in lobby. A Caucasian version of Tokyo Rose. She immediately launched into a description of all the *respectably* employed people who were waiting in line for this apartment. Showed me living room first. Large, airy, terrific view of well-known discount drugstore. Two bedrooms, sure enough. Kitchen, sort of. When I asked why the present occupant had seen fit to cut three five-foot-high arches out of the inside wall of the master bedroom, she muttered something about cross ventilation. When I pointed out that there were no windows on the opposite wall, she ostentatiously extracted a sheaf of papers from her briefcase and studied them closely. Presumably these contained the names of all the Supreme Court Justices who were waiting for this apartment. Nevertheless I pressed on and asked her what one might do with three five-foot-high arches in one's bedroom wall. She suggested stained glass. I suggested pews in the living room and services every Sunday. She showed me a room she referred to as the master bath. I asked her where the slaves bathed. She rustled her papers ominously and showed me the living room again. I

looked disgruntled. She brightened and showed me something called a fun bathroom. It had been covered in fabric
from floor to ceiling by someone who obviously was not
afraid to mix patterns. I informed her unceremoniously that
I never again wanted to be shown a fun bathroom. I don't
want to have fun in the bathroom; I just want to bathe my
slaves.

She showed me the living room again. Either she just
couldn't get enough of that discount drugstore or she was
trying to trick me into thinking there were three living
rooms. Impudently I asked her where one ate, seeing as I
had not been shown a dining room and the kitchen was
approximately the size of a brandy snifter.

"Well," she said, "some people use the second bedroom
as a dining room." I replied that I needed the second bedroom to write in. This was a mistake because it reminded
her of all the ambassadors to the U.N. on her list of prospective tenants.

"Well," she said, "the master bedroom is rather large."

"Listen," I said, "I already eat on my bed. In a one-room,
rent-controlled slum apartment, I'll eat on the bed. In an
ornately priced, high-maintenance co-op, I want to eat at a
table. Call me silly, call me foolish, but that's the kind of girl
I am." She escorted me out of the apartment and left me
standing in the lobby as she hurried off—anxious, no doubt,
to call Cardinal Cooke and tell him okay, the apartment was
his.

Sunday: Spent the entire day recovering from a telephone
call with a real estate broker, who, in response to my having
expressed displeasure at having been shown an apartment in
which the closest thing to a closet had been the living room,

said, "Well, Fran, what do you expect for fourteen hundred a month?" He hung up before I could tell him that actually, to tell you the truth, for fourteen hundred a month I expected the Winter Palace—furnished. Not to mention fully staffed.

Monday: Looked this morning at the top floor of a building which I have privately christened Uncle Tom's Brownstone. One end of the floor sloped sufficiently for me to be able to straighten up and ask why the refrigerator was in the living room. I was promptly put in my place by the owner, who looked me straight in the eye and said, "Because it doesn't fit in the kitchen."

"True," I conceded, taking a closer look, "that is a problem. I'll tell you what, though, and this may not have occurred to you, but that kitchen does fit in the refrigerator. Why don't you try it?"

I left before he could act on my suggestion and repaired to a phone booth. Mortality rate in V.F.'s building still amazingly low.

Called about apartment listed in today's paper. Was told fixture fee $100,000. Replied that unless Rembrandt had doodled on the walls, $100,000 wasn't a fixture fee; it was war reparations.

Tuesday: Let desperation get the best of me and went to see an apartment described as "interesting." "Interesting" generally means that it has a skylight, no elevator and they'll throw in the glassine envelopes for free. This one was even more interesting than usual because, the broker informed me, Jack Kerouac had once lived here. Someone's pulling your leg, I told him; Jack Kerouac's still living here.

Wednesday: Ran into a casual acquaintance on Seventh Avenue. Turns out he too is looking for a two-bedroom apartment. We compared notes.

"Did you see the one with the refrigerator in the living room?" he asked.

"Yes, indeed," I said.

"Well," he said, "today I looked at a dentist's office in the East Fifties."

"A dentist's office," I said. "Was the chair still there?"

"No," he replied, "but there was a sink in every room." It sounded like a deal for someone. I tried to think if I knew of any abortionists looking for a two-bedroom apartment. None sprang to mind.

Called real-estate broker and inquired as to price of newly advertised co-op. Amount in substantial six figures. "What about financing?" I asked.

"Financing?" She shuddered audibly. "This is an all-cash building."

I told her that to me an all-cash building is what you put on Boardwalk or Park Place. She suggested that I look farther uptown. I replied that if I looked any farther uptown I'd have to take karate lessons. She thought that sounded like a good idea.

Thursday: Was shown co-op apartment of recently deceased actor. By now so seasoned that I didn't bat an eye at the sink in the master bedroom. Assumed that either he was a dentist on the side or that it didn't fit in the bathroom. Second assumption proved correct. Couldn't understand why, though; you'd think that there not being a shower in there would have left plenty of room for a sink. Real-estate broker pointed out recent improvements: tangerine-colored kitchen appliances; bronze-mirrored fireplace; a fun living room. Told the broker that what with the asking price, the maintenance and the cost of unimproving, I couldn't afford to live there and still wear shoes on a regular basis.

Called V.F. again. First the good news: a woman in his building died. Then the bad news: she decided not to move.

Fran Lebowitz's
Travel Hints

These hints are the result of exhaustive and painstaking research conducted during a recently completed fourteen-city promotional book tour. This does not mean that if your own travel plans do not include a fourteen-city promotional book tour you should disregard this information. Simply adjust the hints to fit your personal needs, allow for a certain amount of pilot error and you will benefit enormously.

1. It is imperative when flying coach that you restrain any tendency toward the vividly imaginative. For although it may momentarily appear to be the case, it is not at all likely that the cabin is entirely inhabited by crying babies smoking inexpensive domestic cigars.

2. When flying first class, you may frequently need to be reminded of this fact, for it all too often seems that the only discernible difference is that the babies have con-

nections in Cuba. You will, however, be finally reassured when the stewardess drops your drink and the glass breaks.

3. Airplanes are invariably scheduled to depart at such times as 7:54, 9:21 or 11:37. This extreme specificity has the effect on the novice of instilling in him the twin beliefs that he will be *arriving* at 10:08, 1:43 or 4:22, and that he should get to the airport on time. These beliefs are not only erroneous but actually unhealthy, and could easily be dispelled by an attempt on the part of the airlines toward greater realism. Understandably, they may be reluctant to make such a radical change all at once. In an effort to make the transition easier I offer the following graduated alternatives to "Flight 477 to Minneapolis will depart at 8:03 P.M.":

   a. Flight 477 to Minneapolis will depart oh, let's say, eightish.
   b. Flight 477 to Minneapolis will depart around eight, eight-thirty.
   c. Flight 477 to Minneapolis will depart while it's still dark.
   d. Flight 477 to Minneapolis will depart before the paperback is out.

4. Stewardesses are not crazy about girls.

5. Neither are stewards.

6. You *can* change planes in Omaha, Nebraska.

7. You are advised to do so.

8. Whether or not you yourself indulge in the habit, always sit in the smoking section of an airplane. The coughing will break up the trip.

9. Whenever possible, fly with someone who is color-blind. Explaining to him the impact of rust, orange and yellow stripes against a background of aquamarine florals will fill the time you have left over from coughing.

10. When making bookstore appearances in areas heavily populated by artistic types, limit your signing of books "For Douglas and Michael" or "Joseph and Edward" or "Diane and Katy" to under ten copies. It will take you approximately that amount of time to be struck by the realization that you are losing sales. Announce pleasantly but firmly that it is common knowledge that homosexual liaisons are notoriously short-lived, and that eventually there will be a fight over your book. If this fails to have an immediate effect, remind them gently of the number of French whisks they've lost through the years.

11. It's not that it's three hours earlier in California; it's that the days are three hours longer.

12. Room-service menus that don't charge extra for cheese on hamburgers are trying to tell you something.

13. Fleeting romantic alliances in strange cities are acceptable, especially if you've already seen the movie. Just make sure that your companion has gotten the name of your publisher wrong.

14. Local television talk-show hosts are not interested in the information that the *Today* show uses more than one camera.

15. Twenty-four-hour room service generally refers to the length of time that it takes for the club sandwich to arrive. This is indeed disheartening, particularly when you've ordered scrambled eggs.

16. Never relinquish clothing to a hotel valet without first specifically telling him that you want it back.

17. Leaving a wake-up call for four P.M. is certain to result in a loss of respect from the front desk and over-familiarity on the part of bellboys and room-service waiters.

18. If you're going to America, bring your own food.

19. If while staying at a stupendously expensive hotel in Northern California you observe that one of your fellow guests has left his sneakers in front of his door, try to behave yourself.

20. Under no circumstances order from room service an item entitled "The Cheese Festival" unless you are prepared to have your dream of colorfully costumed girls of all nations rolling enormous wheels of Gruyère and Jarlsberg replaced by three Kraft slices and a lot of toothpicks dressed in red cellophane hats.

21. Calling a taxi in Texas is like calling a rabbi in Iraq.

22. Local television talk shows do not, in general, supply make-up artists. The exception to this is Los Angeles,

an unusually generous city in this regard, since they also provide this service for radio appearances.

23. Do not approach with anything even resembling assurance a restaurant that moves.

24. When a newspaper photographer suggests artistically interesting props, risk being impolite.

25. Absolutely, positively, and no matter what, wait until you get back to New York to have your hair cut.

26. Carry cash.

27. Stay inside.

28. Call collect.

29. Forget to write.

Ideas

Ideas

I t was only to be expected that the era that gave us the
word "lifestyle" would sooner or later come up with the
concept of thoughtstyle. Thoughtstyle can probably best be
defined by noting that in the phrase "lifestyle" we have the
perfect example of the total being lesser than the sum of its
parts, since those who use the word "lifestyle" are rarely in
possession of either.

So too with thoughtstyle, and thus we find ourselves the
inhabitants of a period during which ideas are not exactly
flourishing—denizens, in fact, of a time when the most we
can possibly hope to see are a couple of darn good notions.
What is the difference, you may now be asking, between an
idea and a notion? Well, the primary difference, of course,
is that a notion you can sell but an idea you can't even give
away. There are other differences, to be sure, and as can
readily be seen by the following chart, I have taken care not
to neglect them.

IDEAS	NOTIONS
MAKING CHANGE	ALGEBRA
ENGLISH	ESPERANTO
BLUEBERRY PIE	BLUEBERRY VINEGAR
POETRY	POETS
LITERATURE	THE NONFICTION NOVEL
CHOOSING	PICKING
BATHROOMS IN MUSEUMS	PAINTINGS IN BATHROOMS
LIGHT BULBS	LIGHT BEER
THOMAS JEFFERSON	JERRY BROWN
BREAKFAST	BRUNCH
DETROIT	SAUSALITO

While it may appear to the novice that this just about wraps it up, I am afraid that the novice is sadly mistaken. Ideas are, after all, a subject of some complexity. There are good ideas, bad ideas, big ideas, small ideas, old ideas and new ideas. There are ideas that we like and ideas that we don't. But the idea that I have seized upon is the idea that is not quite finished—the idea that starts strong but in the final analysis doesn't quite make it. Naturally, there is more than one such idea, and so I offer what can only be called:

A BUNCH OF HALF-BAKED IDEAS

TRIAL BY A JURY	OF YOUR PEERS
ADULT	EDUCATION
THE NOBLE	SAVAGE
HERO	WORSHIP
IMMACULATE	CONCEPTION
HIGH	TECH
POPULAR	CULTURE
FISCAL	RESPONSIBILITY
SALES	TAX
HUMAN	POTENTIAL
SUPER	MAN
MAY	DAY
BUTCHER	BLOCK
SEXUAL	POLITICS
METHOD	ACTING
MODERN	MEDICINE
LIVING WELL	IS THE BEST REVENGE

When Smoke
Gets in Your Eyes...
Shut Them

As a practicing member of several oppressed minority groups, I feel that I have on the whole conducted myself with the utmost decorum. I have, without exception, refrained from marching, chanting, appearing on *The David Susskind Show* or in any other way making anything that could even vaguely be construed as a fuss. I call attention to this exemplary behavior not merely to cast myself in a favorable light but also to emphasize the seriousness of the present situation. The present situation that I speak of is the present situation that makes it virtually impossible to smoke a cigarette in public without the risk of fine, imprisonment or having to argue with someone not of my class.

Should the last part of that statement disturb the more egalitarian among you, I hasten to add that I use the word "class" in its narrower sense to refer to that group more commonly thought of as "my kind of people." And while there are a great many requirements for inclusion in my kind of people, chief among them is an absolute hands-off policy when it comes to the subject of smoking.

Smoking is, if not my life, then at least my hobby. I love to smoke. Smoking is fun. Smoking is cool. Smoking is, as far as I am concerned, the entire point of being an adult. It makes growing up genuinely worthwhile. I am quite well aware of the hazards of smoking. Smoking is not a healthful pastime, it is true. Smoking is indeed no bracing dip in the ocean, no strenuous series of calisthenics, no two laps around the reservoir. On the other hand, smoking has to its advantage the fact that it is a quiet pursuit. Smoking is, in effect, a dignified sport. Not for the smoker the undue fanfare associated with downhill skiing, professional football or race-car driving. And yet, smoking is—as I have stated previously—hazardous. Very hazardous. Smoking, in fact, is downright dangerous. Most people who smoke will eventually contract a fatal disease and die. But they don't brag about it, do they? Most people who ski, play professional football or drive race cars, will not die—at least not in the act—and yet they are the ones with the glamorous images, the expensive equipment and the mythic proportions. Why this should be I cannot say, unless it is simply that the average American does not know a daredevil when he sees one. And it is the average American to whom I address this discourse because it is the average American who is responsible for the recent spate of no-smoking laws and antismoking sentiment. That it is the average American who must take the blame I have no doubt, for unquestionably the *above-*average American has better things to do.

I understand, of course, that many people find smoking

objectionable. That is their right. I would, I assure you, be the very last to criticize the annoyed. I myself find many—even most—things objectionable. Being offended is the natural consequence of leaving one's home. I do not like aftershave lotion, adults who roller-skate, children who speak French, or anyone who is unduly tan. I do not, however, go around enacting legislation and putting up signs. In private I avoid such people; in public they have the run of the place. I stay at home as much as possible, and so should they. When it is necessary, however, to go out of the house, they must be prepared, as am I, to deal with the unpleasant personal habits of others. That is what "public" means. If you can't stand the heat, get back in the kitchen.

As many of you may be unaware of the full extent of this private interference in the public sector, I offer the following report:

HOSPITALS

Hospitals are, when it comes to the restriction of smoking, perhaps the worst offenders of all. Not only because the innocent visitor must invariably walk miles to reach a smoking area, but also because a hospital is the singularly most illogical place in the world to ban smoking. A hospital is, after all, just the sort of unsavory and nerve-racking environment that makes smoking really pay off. Not to mention that in a hospital, the most frequent objection of the nonsmoker (that *your* smoke endangers *his* health) is rendered entirely meaningless by the fact that everyone there is already sick. Except the visitor—who is not allowed to smoke.

RESTAURANTS

By and large the sort of restaurant that has "no-smoking tables" is just the sort of restaurant that would most benefit from the dulling of its patrons' palates. At the time of this writing, New York City restaurants are still free of this divisive legislation. Perhaps those in power are aware that if the New Yorker was compelled to deal with just one more factor in deciding on a restaurant, there would be a mass return to home cooking. For there is, without question, at least in my particular circle, not a single person stalwart enough, after a forty-minute phone conversation, when everyone has finally and at long last agreed on Thai food, downtown, at 9:30, to then bear up under the pressures inherent in the very idea of smoking and no-smoking tables.

MINNESOTA

Due to something called the Minnesota Clean Air Act, it is illegal to smoke in the baggage-claim area of the Minneapolis Airport. This particular bit of news is surprising, since it has been my personal observation that even non-smokers tend to light up while waiting to see if their baggage has accompanied them to their final destination. As I imagine that this law has provoked a rather strong response, I was initially quite puzzled as to why Minnesota would risk alienating what few visitors it had been able to attract. This mystery was cleared up when, after having spent but a single day there, I realized that in Minnesota the Clean Air Act is a tourist attraction. It may not be the Beaubourg, but it's

all their own. I found this to be an interesting, subtle concept, and have suggested to state officials that they might
further exploit its commercial possibilities by offering for
sale plain blue postcards emblazoned with the legend:
Downtown Minneapolis.

AIRPLANES

Far be it from me to incite the general public by rashly
suggesting that people who smoke are smarter than people
who don't. But I should like to point out that I number
among my acquaintances not a single nicotine buff who
would entertain, for even the briefest moment, the notion
that sitting six inches in front of a smoker is in any way
healthier than sitting six inches behind him.

TAXICABS

Perhaps one of the most chilling features of New York life
is hearing the meter click in a taxicab before one has noticed
the sign stating: PLEASE DO NOT SMOKE DRIVER ALLERGIC.
One can, of course, exercise the option of disembarking
immediately should one not mind being out a whole dollar,
or one can, more thriftily, occupy oneself instead by attempting to figure out just how it is that a man who cannot
find his way from the Pierre Hotel to East Seventy-eighth
Street has somehow managed to learn the English word for
allergic.

The Last Laugh

Coming from a family where literary tradition runs largely toward the picture postcard, it is not surprising that I have never really succeeded in explaining to my grandmother exactly what it is that I do. It is not that my grandmother is unintelligent; quite the contrary. It is simply that so firmly implanted are her roots in retail furniture that she cannot help but view all other occupations from this rather limited vantage point. Therefore, every time I see my grandmother I am fully prepared for the following exchange:

"So, how are you?"

"Fine, Grandma. How are you?"

"Fine. So how's business, good?"

"Very good, Grandma."

"You busy this time of year? Is this a good season for you?"

"Very good, Grandma."

"Good. It's good to be busy."

"Yes, Grandma."

Satisfied with my responses, my grandmother will then turn to my father and ask the very same questions, a dialogue a bit more firmly grounded in reality, since he has not deviated from the Lebowitz custom of fine upholstered furniture.

The lack of understanding between my grandmother and myself has long troubled me, and in honor of her recently celebrated ninety-fifth birthday I have prepared the following business history in order that she might have a clearer vision of my life and work.

My beginnings were humble, of course, but I am not ashamed of them. I started with a humor pushcart on Delancey Street—comic essays, forty cents apiece, four for a dollar. It was tough out there on the street; competition was cutthroat, but it was the best education in the world because on Delancey "mildly amusing" was not enough—you had to be *funny*. I worked ten-hour days, six days a week, and soon I had a nice little following. Not exactly a cult, maybe, but I was doing okay. It was a living. I was able to put aside some money, and things looked pretty good for a store of my own in the not too distant future. Oh sure, I had my troubles, who doesn't? The housewives browsing through every essay on the cart, trying to contain their glee in the hope that I'd come down a little in price. The kids snitching a couple of paragraphs when my back was turned. And Mike the cop with his hand out all the time looking for a free laugh. But I persevered, never losing sight of my objective, and after years of struggle I was ready to take the plunge.

I went down to Canal Street to look for a store, a store of my own. Not being one to do things halfway, I was thorough and finally found a good location. Lots of foot traffic, surgical supplies on one side, maternity clothes on the other—these were people who could use a good laugh. I worked like a dog getting ready for that opening. I put in a very reasonable ready-to-hear line, an amusing notions counter, a full stock of epigrams, aphorisms and the latest in wit and irony. At last I was ready; Fran's Humor Heaven: Home of the Devastating Double Entendre was open for business. It was tough going at first, but my overhead was low. I wrote all my own stock. And eventually I began to show a nice healthy gross and a net I could live with.

I don't know when it all began to go sour—who can tell about these things, I'm a humorist, not a fortuneteller—but business began to slip. First I took a bath with some barbed comments I was trying out, and then I got stuck with a lot of entertaining anecdotes. I hoped it was just an off season, but it didn't let up, and before I knew it I was in really big trouble. I tried everything, believe you me. I ran big sales— "Buy one epigram, get one free," "Twenty percent off all phrases." I even instituted a "Buy now, say later" plan. But nothing worked. I was at my wits' end; I owed everybody and was in hock up to my ears. So one day, pen in hand, I went to Morris "The Thesaurus" Pincus—a shy on East Houston who lent money to humorists in a jam. The interest rates were exorbitant but I signed my life away. What else could I do?

But it wasn't enough, and I was forced to take in a collaborator. At first he seemed to be working out. He specialized in parodies and they were moving pretty good, but before too long I began to get suspicious of him. I mean, I could barely put food on my table, and there he was, riding around in a Cadillac a block long. One night after dinner I went back to the store and went over the books with a fine-tooth comb. Just as I thought, there it was in black and white: the guy was a thief. He'd been stealing my lines all along. I confronted him with the evidence and what could he do? He promised to pay me back a few pages a week, but I knew that was one joker I'd never see again.

I kicked him out and worked even harder. Eighty-hour weeks, open every night until ten, but it was a losing battle. With the big humor chains moving in, what chance did an independent like me have? Then the day came when I knew all was lost. Sol's Discount Satire opened up right across the street. He wrote in bulk; I couldn't meet his prices. I, of course, was wittier, but nobody cared about quality anymore. Their attitude was "So it's a little broad, but at forty percent below list we'll forsake a little subtlety." I went in the back of the store and sat down, trying desperately to figure something out. There was a sharp rap at the door, and in walked Morris, a goon on either side, ready to collect. I told him I didn't have it. I begged for more time. I was pleading for my life. Morris stared at me coolly, a hard glint in his eye as he cleaned his nails with a lethal-looking fountain pen.

"Look, Fran," he said, "you're breaking my heart. Either you pay up by next Monday, or I'm gonna spread it around that you're mixing your metaphors."

With that he turned on his heel and walked out the door followed by the two gorillas. I was sweating bullets. If Morris spread that around, I'd never get another laugh as long as I lived. My head swam with crazy plans, and when I realized what I had to do, my heart thumped like a jackhammer.

Late that night I went back to the store. I let myself in through the side door and set to work. I poured a lot of gasoline around, took a last look, threw in a match and beat it the hell out of there. I was twenty blocks away when the full realization of what I'd done hit me. Overcome by remorse, I ran all the way back, but it was too late. The deed was done; I'd burned my comic essays for the insurance money.

The next day I met with the adjuster from That's Life, and thank God he bought the fire and paid me off. It was just enough to settle with Morris, and then I was broke again.

I started to free-lance for other stores, writing under a pseudonym, of course. My heart wasn't in it, but I needed the cash. I was grinding it out like hamburger meat, trying to build up some capital. The stuff was too facile, I knew that, but there was a market for it, so I made the best of it.

The years went by and I was just getting to the point where I could take it a little easy, when I was struck by an idea that was to change not only my own life but that of everyone in the entire humor business. The idea? Fast humor. After all, the pace had picked up a lot since my days on Delancey Street. The world was a different place; humor habits had changed. Everyone was in a hurry. Who had time anymore for a long comic essay, a slow build, a good long laugh? Everything was rush, rush, rush. Fast humor was an idea whose time had come.

Once again I started small, just a little place out on Queens Boulevard. I called it Rapid Repartee and used every modern design technique available. All chrome and glass, everything sleek and clean. Known in the business for my cunning and waggish ways, I couldn't resist a little joke and so used as my trademark a golden arch. No one got it. So I added another one, and got a great reaction. You really have to hit people over the head, don't you? Be that as it may, the place caught on like wildfire. I couldn't keep Quick Comebacks in stock, and the Big Crack was the hit of the century. I began to franchise, but refused to relinquish qual-

ity control. Business boomed and today I can tell you I'm
sitting pretty. I've got it all: a penthouse on Park, a yacht
the size of the *Queen Mary* and a Rolls you could live in.
But still, every once in a while I get that old creative itch.
When this happens I slip on an apron and cap, step behind
one of my thousands of counters, smile pleasantly at the
customer and say, "Good morning. Something nice in a
Stinging Barb?" If I'm recognized, it's always good for a
laugh, because, believe you me, in this business unless you
have a sense of humor you're dead.

The Fran Lebowitz
High Stress Diet
and Exercise Program

E ach year millions of people attempt to shed excess
pounds by dint of strenuous diet and exercise. They
nibble carrot sticks, avoid starches, give up drinking, run
around reservoirs, lift weights, swing from trapezes and otherwise behave in a manner that suggests an unhappy penchant for undue fanfare. All of this is, of course, completely
unnecessary, for it is entirely possible—indeed, easy—to lose
weight and tone up without the slightest effort of will. One
has merely to conduct one's life in such a way that pounds
and inches will disappear as of their own volition.

Magic, you say? Fantasy? Pie in the sky? Longing of the

basest sort? Not at all, I assure you, not at all. No magic, no fantasy, no dreamy hopes of any kind. But a secret, ah yes, there is a secret. The secret of exploiting an element present in everyone's daily life, and using to its fullest advantage the almost inexhaustible resources available within.

That element? Stress. Yes, stress; plain, ordinary, every-day stress. The same type of stress that everyone has handy at any time of the day or night. Call it what you will: annoyance, work, pressure, art, love, it is stress nevertheless, and it is stress that will be your secret weapon as you embark on my foolproof program of physical fitness and bodily beauty.

DIET

The downfall of most diets is that they restrict your intake of food. This is, of course, galling, and inevitably leads to failure. The Fran Lebowitz High Stress Diet (T.F.L.H.S.D. for short) allows unlimited quantities of all foods. You may eat whatever you like. If you can choke it down, it's yours. The following is a partial list of allowed foods. Naturally, space limitations make it impossible to furnish a complete list. If you can eat something that is not on this list—good luck to you.

Allowed Foods

Meat	Candy	Rice
Fish	Nuts	Spaghetti
Fowl	Cereal	Sugar
Eggs	Cookies	Syrup
Cheese	Crackers	Pizza

Butter	Honey	Potato Chips
Cream	Ice Cream	Pretzels
Mayonnaise	Ketchup	Pie
Fruits	Jam	Wine
Vegetables	Macaroni	Liquor
Bread	Milk	Beer
Cake	Pancakes	Ale

As you can see, T.F.L.H.S.D. permits you a variety of foods unheard of on most diets. And, as I have stated previously, quantity is of no concern. I ask only that you coordinate your eating with specific physical activities. This program is detailed below.

EQUIPMENT

You can proceed with The Fran Lebowitz High Stress Exercise Program (T.F.L.H.S.E.P.) without the purchase of special equipment; it calls for only those accouterments that you undoubtedly possess already. A partial list follows:

Cigarettes
Matches or lighter
A career
One or more lawyers
One agent or manager
At least one, but preferably two, extremely complicated
   love affairs
A mailing address
Friends
Relatives
A landlord

Necessary equipment will, of course, vary from person to person, but T.F.L.H.S.E.P. is flexible and can adapt to almost any situation. This is clearly seen in the sample one-day menu and exercise program that follows. It must be remembered that it is absolutely mandatory that you follow exercise instructions while eating.

Sample Menu and Program

BREAKFAST

Large Orange Juice
6 Pancakes with Butter, Syrup and/or Jam
4 Slices Bacon and/or 4 Sausage Links
Coffee with Cream and Sugar
11 Cigarettes

a. Take first bite of pancake.
b. Call agent. Discover that in order to write screenplay you must move to Los Angeles for three months and enter into a collaboration with a local writer who has to his credit sixteen episodes of *The Partridge Family*, one unauthorized biography of Ed McMahon, and the novelization of the projected sequel to *Missouri Breaks*. (Excellent for firming jawline.)

MIDMORNING SNACK

2 Glazed Doughnuts
Coffee with Cream and Sugar
8 Cigarettes

a.   Take first sip of coffee.
b.   Open mail and find final disconnect notice from tele-
     phone company, threatening letter from spouse of new
     flame and a note from a friend informing you that you
     have been recently plagiarized on network television.
     (Tones up fist area.)

LUNCH

   2 Vodka and Tonics
   Chicken Kiev
   Pumpernickel Bread and Butter
   Green Salad
   White Wine
   A Selection or Selections from the Pastry Tray
   Coffee with Cream and Sugar
   15 Cigarettes

a.   Arrange to lunch with lawyer.
b.   Take first bite of Chicken Kiev.
c.   Inquire of lawyer as to your exact chances in litigation
     against CBS. (Flattens tummy fast.)

DINNER

   3 Vodka and Tonics
   Spaghetti al Pesto
   Veal Piccata
   Zucchini
   Arugula Salad
   Cheese Cake

Coffee with Cream and Sugar
Brandy
22 Cigarettes

a. Arrange to dine with small group that includes three
    people with whom you are having clandestine love
    affairs, your younger sister from out of town, a business
    rival to whom you owe a great deal of money and two
    of the lawyers from CBS. It is always more fruitful to
    exercise with others. (Tightens up the muscles.)

As I have said, this is just a sample, and any combination
of foods and exercises will work equally well. Your daily
weight loss should average from between three to five
pounds, depending largely on whether you are smoking a
sufficient number of cigarettes. This is a common pitfall and
close attention should be paid, for inadequate smoking is
certain to result in a lessening of stress. For those of you who
simply cannot meet your quota, it is imperative that you
substitute other exercises, such as moving in downstairs
from an aspiring salsa band and/or being terribly frank with
your mother. If these methods fail, try eating while reading
the *New York Times* Real Estate section. Admittedly, this
is a drastic step and should not be taken before you have first
warmed up with at least six pages of Arts and Leisure and
one sexual encounter with a person vital to your career.

Occasionally I run across a dieter with an unusually stub-
born weight problem. If you fall into this category, I recommend as a final desperate measure that you take your meals
with a magazine editor who really and truly understands
your work and a hairdresser who wants to try something new
and interesting.

The Unnatural Order

New Yorkers whose formative years were spent in more rural environments are frequently troubled by their inability to spot seasonal change. Deprived of such conventional signs as caterpillars, yellow leaves and the frost on the pumpkin, these bewildered citizens are quarterly confronted with the problem of ascertaining just exactly when it is what time of year. In an attempt to dispel this sort of confusion I offer the following guide:

AUTUMN

Autumn refers to the period beginning in late September and ending right before January. Its most salient visual characteristic is that white people all over town begin to lose their tans. New Yorkers, however, being somewhat reserved, it is not good form to try to rake them up and jump in them. Recent air-pollution control laws have also prohibited their burning, no matter how nostalgic one is for the homey scent of a roaring bonfire. Another marked feature of this season, and one not unrelated to the aforementioned, is that there *are* white people all over town, a fact worth noting in this context as it signals a mass return from the Hamptons (see Summer).

Nubbier, more textured fabrics start to make an appearance and shoes begin gradually to become more bootlike.

Politicians begin to spout brightly hued wild promises, but it is unwise to pick them, particularly early in the season, and on the whole one is far safer in sticking to the cultivated varieties.

WINTER

Winter begins where autumn leaves off, but has a lot more staying power than its quicksilver antecedent. As this season progresses one begins again to note fewer white people on the street (see Barbados) and more black people on television (see landlord's attitudes toward supplying heat; see landlords in person in Barbados).

Outdoor fashion shootings become sparse and are replaced by illegal aliens selling outsized pretzels and cold chestnuts.

Due to the dangers of the chill air, buses tend to band together in herds and Checker cabs pair off and retire to their garages for mutual warmth and companionship.

Although the frozen ground is hard and unyielding, often city contracts covering vital services come up for renewal (see Autumn, Spring and Summer) and mayoral press conferences are abundant.

Along about February, literary agents begin to turn green while talking on the telephone to their cinematic counterparts, and almost as one fly West to negotiate. Shortly after their return they will begin to lose their tans, but this is merely an example of the exception proving the rule and should not be taken by the novice as a sign of autumn. It is still winter, so try to regain your bearings by determining which out-of-season fruits are the most expensive.

SPRING

Rumored to be a season separating winter and summer, spring is, in New York, a rather mythical figure, and as such attracts a slightly rarefied crowd. Around April, art directors and aesthetic realists begin shedding their sweaters, and very constructed young men start to plan next autumn's colors. Property values on eastern Long Island rise sharply (see white people), while the level of reason and good will recedes from the banks.

Newsstands become more delicately tinged as magazine covers once again sport their seasonal pastel look and the word "relationship" is in the air, although fortunately not in the water.

Along about May, movie agents in Los Angeles begin to turn green while on the telephone to their literary counterparts and as one fly East to negotiate. Shortly after their arrival they will begin to lose their tans, but this will compel them to leave before even the rawest novice can think that it's autumn.

SUMMER

Although the most hard-nosed element maintains that summer is that time which is not winter, it technically describes the interval between spring and autumn, and most quickly manifests itself by a luxuriant growth in Con Edison bills.

The air becomes more visible, and a great many adults, stunned by the bountiful harvest of roving street gangs and sidewalk domino players, forget that they look terrible in shorts. Daylight-saving time blossoms once more and is welcomed heartily by insomniacs who now have less night to be up all of.

Wits thicken, urban flesh turns a vivid gray and the word "relationship" is in the water, but not, fortunately, in the city.

How to Be
a Directory Assistance
Operator: A Manual

INTRODUCTION

Uppermost in your mind should be the fact that as a Directory Assistance Operator your job is to serve the public. You must be helpful and courteous, of course, but serving the public is a grave responsibility and consists of a good deal more than might be immediately apparent. Give them the number, sure, but it must be remembered that the public is made up largely of people, and that people have needs far beyond mere telephone numbers. Modern life is such that the public has come to rely rather heavily on convenience, often forgetting the value and rewards of difficult, sustained labor. The human animal has an instinctive need for challenge, and you, as a Directory Assistance Operator, can be instrumental in reintroducing this factor to the lives of your charges. So serve the public, by all means, but do not make the mistake of thinking that serving the public compels you to indulge its every whim—for that, future Directory Assistance Operator, would be not only an error in perception but also a tacit admission of irresponsibility.

LESSON ONE: IS THAT A BUSINESS OR A RESIDENCE?

When a member of the public (henceforth to be referred to as the Caller) asks you for a number, do not even think about looking it up before you have inquired in a pleasant yet firm tone of voice, "Is that a business or a residence?" This procedure is never to be omitted, for doing so would display an improper and quite unforgivable presumptuousness on your part. Just because the Russian Tea Room doesn't sound like someone's name to *you* doesn't mean that it isn't. Americans *often* have strange names, a fact that has no doubt come to your attention no matter how short a time you may have been in our country.

LESSON TWO: DO YOU HAVE THE ADDRESS?

This lesson is of primary importance as it serves a twofold purpose. The first of these is to facilitate the process of finding the number in cases where there are many parties with the same name. Note that this is not the case in the aforementioned Russian Tea Room, who seems, poor man, to have no living relatives, at least not in Manhattan. The second and more important reason for asking this question is to make certain that the Caller is really interested in the *telephone number,* and is not imposing on your time and energy in a sneaky attempt to weasel out of you, the Directory Assistance Operator, an exact street address. You are, after all, employed by the New York Telephone Company, and are not under any circumstances to allow yourself to be badly used by some larcenous Caller trying to pull a fast one.

LESSON THREE: COULD YOU SPELL THAT, PLEASE?

The Caller will frequently respond to this query with an audible and unpleasant sigh, or in extreme cases an outright expletive. Ignore him absolutely. You are just doing your job, and anyway, what good reason could he possibly have for wanting to telephone someone whose name he won't or can't even spell?

LESSON FOUR: IS THAT "B" AS IN BOY?

In recent times this traditional, even classic, question has presented a rather touchy problem. Marches have been marched, laws have been passed, rights have been won. The sensitivity of the average member of the Third World has been heightened to the point where asking, no matter how respectfully, "Is that 'B' as in boy?" is apt to provoke an unseemly response. But since it is quite impossible, no matter how empathetic one may be, to logically inquire, "Is that 'B' as in man?," the modern Directory Assistance Operator is pretty much on her own here. Do, however, avoid "Is that 'B' as in black?" because you can never tell these days. And times being what they are, male Directory Assistance Opera-tors assisting female callers are cautioned strongly against even thinking of risking, "Is that 'B' as in baby?"

LESSON FIVE: YOU CAN FIND THAT NUMBER LISTED IN YOUR DIRECTORY

This last procedure, coming as it does at the end of your long, often stressful association with the Caller, is the one most commonly neglected, particularly by the novice. Its importance should, however, not be underestimated, as it is well known that last impressions are lasting impressions. The Directory Assistance Operator is, as has been frequently illustrated in this manual, subjected to every sort of unattractive and condescending human behavior. "You can find that number listed in your directory" is your opportunity to establish once and for all that the Directory Assistance Operator is nobody's fool. "You can find that number listed in your directory" lets the Caller know, in no uncertain terms, that you have no intention of being pushed around by *anyone,* let alone anyone who, it seems, cannot even read the telephone book. So, for heaven's sake, never forget "You can find that number listed in your directory." It gets them every time.

ADDENDUM: HAVE A NICE DAY

The truly dedicated Directory Assistance Operator never fails to conclude the call with a sprightly rendition of "Have a nice day." "Have a nice day" is the perfect parting shot, not only because it shows once and for all which of you is the bigger person, but also because it has the eminently satisfying effect of causing the Caller to forget the number.

War Stories

D espite my strenuous, not to say unparalleled, efforts to remain ill-informed, it has come to my attention that there has been, of late, some talk of war. Discussions concerning the drafting of women, the enrichment of the defense budget, and a certain unease on the part of older teenagers has led me to assume that what you people have in mind here is a regular war with soldiers, as opposed to a modern war with buttons.

Being classically inclined, I applaud this apparent return to the tried and true, yet cannot help but feel that contemporary life has taken its toll and we will thus be compelled to make certain allowances and institute practices that can only be called unorthodox. It is, therefore, in the national interests of a smooth transition and eventual victory that I offer the following:

SUPPOSE THEY GAVE A WAR AND YOU WEREN'T INVITED

The first step in having any successful war is getting people to fight it. You can have the biggest battlefields on your bloc, the best artillery money can buy and strategies galore, but without those all-important combat troops your war just won't get started. Numbers alone are not enough, however, and many a country has made the mistake of filling its armed forces with too many of the same type. A good mix is essential. Monotony is as dangerous on the battlefield as it is on the highway. The problem, then, is how to attract the sort of large and varied group that you are going to need.

The draft, of course, is traditional and always appropriate but it has, in recent years, fallen somewhat out of favor, becoming in the process not only old hat but downright ineffective. Clearly, extreme measures are called for, and in no way could they be better served than by the implementation of just a touch of psychological warfare. By combining the aforementioned situation with the indisputable fact that the grass is always greener on the other side of the fence, I suggest that instead of drafting, the powers that be consider inviting. Inviting ensures attendance by all but the most conscientious of objectors, who are impossible to get for really big things anyway. And although inviting might, at first glance, appear to be rather a grand gesture, the actual invitations can and should be simple and functional. Engraved invitations are showy, unduly formal and altogether lacking in urgency. The desired effect can probably best be achieved by the prudent use of the Mailgram. With the invitee's name and address in the upper left-hand corner a personal salutation is unnecessary.

We then proceed to the body of the Mailgram, which might, for example, read:

YOU ARE CORDIALLY INVITED TO
ATTEND THE ONLY PREDECLARATION

INDUCTION INTO THE ARMY FOR THE
UNITED STATES OF AMERICA'S
FORTHCOMING WAR. THE INDUCTION
WILL BEGIN PROMPTLY AT 8:00 A.M. AT
201 VARICK STREET, NEW YORK CITY ON
APRIL 15. WE REGRET THAT DUE TO
LIMITED SPACE ONLY ONE PERSON CAN
BE ADMITTED PER INVITATION.

R.S.V.P. TO OUR OFFICES ON OR BEFORE
MARCH 30. YOUR NAME ON OUR R.S.V.P.
LIST WILL EXPEDITE YOUR ADMISSION.

THIS INVITATION IS NOT TRANSFERABLE.

Only one person can be admitted per invitation? This
invitation is not transferable? Talk about impact. Imagine,
if you will, the days immediately following the receipt of this
missive. You are one of the lucky ones. There are others less
fortunate. First casual inquiries, then pointed requests,
finally desperate begging. On the eve of the induction the
truly insecure go out of town while the aggressively defen-
sive announce that they're exhausted and have decided to
just stay in and order Chinese food. Yes, people will be hurt.
Friendships will be dissolved. New, decidedly unappealing
alliances will be formed. It's too bad, but it can't be helped.
Blood, sweat and tears are no longer enough; nowadays you
need a door policy. All is fair in love and war.

THE CHILDREN'S CRUSADE

The most recent official statements on the subject indicate
that when it comes to war, the powers that be are partial

to eighteen- and nineteen-year-olds. The parents of these youths may understandably be disconcerted at having to send their children off to what is at best an unfamiliar environment. In an effort to assuage these fears, I suggest that they think of the army as simply another kind of summer camp, and keep in mind that their child may well be the one to return with that highest of honors: Best All-Around Soldier.

Camp Base

For Boys and Girls Ages 18–19
■   Our 102nd season as a friendly, caring community   ■   Complete facilities   ■   Hiking   ■   Riflery   ■ Overnight trips   ■   Backpacking ■   Radar

EXTRA SPECIAL FORCES

Being in my absolute latest possible twenties, I am not myself of draftable age. That does not mean, though, that I am entirely without patriotism and the attendant desire to serve my country.

Desire is not, however (at least in this instance), synonymous with fanaticism, and I do feel that those of us who choose to go should receive certain privileges and considerations. The kinds of certain privileges and considerations I had in mind were these: either I go right from the start as a general or they establish, along guidelines set down by me, a Writers' Regiment.

Guidelines Set Down by Me

a. War is, undoubtedly, hell, but there is no earthly reason why it has to start so early in the morning. Writers, on the whole, find it difficult to work during the day; it is far too distracting. The writer is an artist, a creative person; he needs time to think, to read, to ruminate. Ruminating in particular is not compatible with reveille. Instead, next to each (double) bed in the Writers' Barracks (or suites, as they are sometimes called) should be a night table minimally equipped with an ashtray, a refreshing drink, a good reading lamp and a telephone. Promptly at 1:30 P.M. the phone may ring and a pleasant person with a soft voice may transmit the wake-up call.

b. In the army, discipline must, of course, be maintained and generally this is accomplished by a chain of command. In a chain of command you have what is known as the superior officer. The superior officer is fine for ordinary soldiers such as lighting designers and art directors, but the Writers' Regiment would, by definition, require instead something a bit different: the superior prose stylist. Having a superior prose stylist would, I am sure, be an acceptable, even welcome, policy, and will without question be adopted just as soon as the first writer meets one.

c. The members of the Writers' Regiment would, of course, like to join the rest of you in dangerous armed combat, but unfortunately the pen is mightier than the sword and we must serve where we are needed.

INTERNATIONAL ARRIVALS

Traditionally, former U.S. Air Force pilots have sought and attained employment with the commercial airlines. Today we can look forward to a reversal of this custom, as the U.S. Air Force becomes the recipient of commercially trained airline personnel:

"Hello, this is your captain, Skip Dietrich, speaking. It's nice to have you aboard. We're going to be entering a little enemy fire up ahead and you may experience some slight discomfort. The temperature in the metro Moscow area is twenty below zero and it's snowing. We're a little behind schedule on account of that last hit, so we should be arriving at around two-thirty Their Time. Those of you in the tourist cabin seated on the right-hand side of the plane might want to glance out the window and catch what's left of the wing before it goes entirely. That's about all for now, hope you have a pleasant flight and thank you for flying United States Air Force."

The Short Form

The poor are, on the whole, an unhappy lot. Ofttimes cold, invariably short of cash, frequently hungry, they unquestionably have grounds for complaint and few would dispute this. In general, the poor are deprived of most of the things that comprise that which is called "the good life" or "the American standard of living." This state of affairs has been duly noted by both the government and the governed, and much has been done in an attempt to alleviate the situation. Wherever a lack has been perceived a solution has been proposed. No money? Welfare. No apartment? Public housing. No breakfast? Food stamps. No tickee? No washee. No, that's another story. At any rate, you get my drift. The poor need help. The unpoor are willing —some, excessively so.

For those unpoor genuinely dedicated to good works it should come as no surprise that the dilemma of the poor extends far beyond that of the material. Lest you jump to conclusions, I should like to make immediately clear that I am not about to expound on the universal human need for love and affection. As far as I can tell, the poor get all the love and affection they can possibly handle. The concept of an unsuitable marriage obviously started somewhere.

No, I am not speaking here of emotional needs, but rather of those of a social nature. Needs of a social nature are perhaps the most complex and painful to discuss; yet they must be dealt with.

In order that you might gain a better understanding of this matter, I offer by way of illustration an imaginary dinner party (the very best kind) given by a member of the unpoor for his peers, you among them. You choose to accompany you a needy friend. He lacks the proper attire. You accommodate him from your own wardrobe. Your host provides ample food and drink. Your friend is momentarily happy. He feels unpoor, you feel generous, your host feels gracious, good will abounds. For just an instant, you toy with the notion that poverty could be completely eradicated by the simple act of including the poor in the dinner plans of the unpoor. Coffee is served. The talk becomes earnest. The conversation, as is its wont, turns to tax problems.

It is at this point, I assure you, that as far as the poor on your left is concerned, the party is over. Suddenly he feels poor again. Worse than poor—left out. He has no tax problems. He is, as they say, disenfranchised, dispossessed, an outcast, not in the mainstream. And under the present system he will remain in this degrading position for the life of his poverty. The double whammy. As long as he is poor he will be without tax problems, and as long as he is without tax problems he will, let us not forget, also be without tax benefits. And they call this a democracy. A democracy, when one man is in a fifty percent bracket and his dinner companion is in no bracket at all. It isn't enough that a man has no food, no clothing, no roof over his head. No, he also has no accountant, no investment lawyer, no deductions, no loopholes. And very likely no receipts.

This is, of course, unconscionable, and now that you have been apprised of the situation, it is unthinkable that it go on one minute longer—certainly not if we are to call our society an equitable one. Fortunately, there is a solution to this problem, startling in its simplicity, and one that should be implemented immediately.

Tax the poor. Heavily. No halfway measures. No crumbs from the rich man's table. I mean *tax*. Fifty percent bracket, property, capital gains, inheritance—the works.

Now, it has probably occurred to the careful (or even slovenly) reader that somehow this doesn't quite jibe. Something is amiss, you may say. The point you will be quick to raise is that the poor lack the means to be taxed. They cannot afford it. But I am ready for you, and will counter by saying that your inability to accept my solution is a matter of scale, of relativity. Let us examine each point separately.

FIFTY PERCENT

This is, naturally, the easiest to grasp, for it should be quite apparent to all that everyone has half, the poor included. If someone makes even as little as $1,000 a year, this still leaves him $500 for income taxes. Not a fortune, certainly, but still nothing to sneeze at.

PROPERTY

Your difficulty here is undoubtedly conceptual. That is, your conception of property very likely tends toward that fallow acreage, midtown real estate, principal residence sort of thing. It is true, of course, that these are all fine examples of property, but in a democracy who among us would deep down consider it really quite cricket to limit the definition of property to just the fine examples? After all, property merely means ownership; that which one owns is one's property. Therefore property taxes could—and should—easily be levied against the property of the poor. Equal freedom, equal responsibility. So no more free rides for hot plates, vinyl outerwear or electric space heaters.

CAPITAL GAINS

Now, this one is tricky but not insurmountable. And not surprisingly, the dictionary comes in handy. *Webster's Unabridged Second Edition.* The definition of "capital": *This accumulated stock of the product of former labor is termed capital.* And for "capital gains": *Profit resulting from the sale of capital investments, as stock, etc.* There, see? Another instance of relativity. Now. Uh. Yes. Um. Uh. Oh, all right, I admit it: it probably won't come up that often. But the poor would be well advised not to try selling off any leftover Spam Bake without reporting it.

INHERITANCE

Being creatures of habit, we ordinarily associate inheritance with death. Strictly speaking, we need not do so. Once again the dictionary proves most useful when it yields as a definition of "inherit": *To come into possession as an heir or successor.* Successor is, of course, they key word here. Thus, we can plainly see that while to some the word "inherit" may conjure up images of venerable country estates and square-cut emeralds, to others—i.e., the poor—quite differ-ent visions spring to mind. A hand-me-down pair of Dacron slacks is, of course, no square-cut emerald, but then again, five hundred dollars is, as I believe I mentioned in point number one, not a fortune, certainly.

An Alphabet
of New Year's Resolutions
for Others

As an answering-service operator, I will make every effort when answering a subscriber's telephone to avoid sighing in a manner which suggests that in order to answer said telephone I have been compelled to interrupt extremely complicated neurological surgery, which is, after all, my real profession.

Being on the short side and no spring chicken to boot, I shall refrain in perpetuity from anything even roughly akin to leather jodhpurs.

Chocolate chip cookies have perhaps been recently overvalued. I will not aggravate the situation further by opening yet another cunningly named store selling these items at prices more appropriate to a semester's tuition at Harvard Law School.

Despite whatever touch of color and caprice they might indeed impart, I will never, never, *never* embellish my personal written correspondence with droll little crayoned drawings.

Even though I am breathtakingly bilingual, I will not attempt ever again to curry favor with waiters by asking for the wine list in a studiously insinuating tone of French.

Four inches is not a little trim; my job as a hairdresser makes it imperative that I keep this in mind.

Gifted though I might be with a flair for international politics, I will renounce the practice of exhibiting this facility to my passengers.

However ardently I am implored, I pledge never to divulge whatever privileged information I have been able to acquire from my very close friend who stretches canvas for a famous artist.

In light of the fact that I am a frequent, not to say permanent, fixture at even the most obscure of public events, I hereby vow to stop once and for all telling people that I never go out.

Just because I own my own restaurant does not mean that I can include on the menu a dish entitled Veal Jeffrey.

Kitchens are not suitable places in which to install wall-to-wall carpeting, no matter how industrial, how highly technical, how very dark gray. I realize this now.

Large pillows, no matter how opulently covered or engagingly and generously scattered about, are not, alas, furniture. I will buy a sofa.

May lightning strike me dead on the spot should I ever again entertain the notion that anyone is interested in hearing what a fabulously warm and beautiful people I found the Brazilians to be when I went to Rio for Carnival last year.

No hats.

Overeating in expensive restaurants and then writing about it with undue enthusiasm is not at all becoming. I will get a real job.

Polite conversation does not include within its peripheries questions concerning the whereabouts of that very sweet mulatto dancer he was with the last time you saw him.

Quite soon I will absolutely stop using the word "brilliant" in reference to the accessories editors of European fashion magazines.

Raspberries, even out of season, are not a controlled substance. As a restaurant proprietor I have easy, legal access. I will be more generous.

S uccess is something I will dress for when I get there, and not until. Cross my heart and hope to die.

T ies, even really, really narrow ones, are just not enough. I will try to stop relying on them quite so heavily.

U nless specifically requested to do so, I will not discuss Japanese science-fiction movies from the artistic point of view.

V iolet will be a good color for hair at just about the same time that brunette becomes a good color for flowers. I will not forget this.

W hen approached for advice on the subject of antique furniture, I will respond to all queries with reason and decorum so as not to ally myself with the sort of overbred collector who knows the value of everything and the price of nothing.

X is not a letter of the alphabet that lends itself easily, or even with great difficulty, to this type of thing. I promise not to even try.

Y outh, at least in New York City, is hardly wasted on the young. They make more than sufficient use of it. I cannot afford to overlook this.

Z elda Fitzgerald, fascinating as she undoubtedly appears to have been, I promise to cease emulating immediately.

To Have and Do Not

Not too long ago a literary agent of my close acquaintance negotiated a book deal on behalf of a writer of very successful commercial fiction. The book in question has not yet been written. At all. Not one page. On the basis, however, of the reputation of the author and the expertise of the agent, the book-to-be was sold for the gratifying sum of one million dollars. The following week the same agent sold the same book *manqué* for the exact same figure to, as they say, the movies.

Soon thereafter I found myself seated at dinner beside the fellow who had purchased the movie rights to the book in question. I smiled at him politely. He smiled back. I broached the subject.

"I understand," said I, "that you have purchased A Writer of Very Successful Commercial Fiction's next book for one million dollars?"

"Yes," he said. "Why don't *you* write a movie for us?"

I explained that my schedule could not, at this time,

accommodate such a task, seeing as how I was up to my ears in oversleeping, unfounded rumors and superficial friendships. We were silent for a moment. We ate. We drank. I had an idea.

"You just bought A Writer of Very Successful Commercial Fiction's unwritten book for one million dollars, right?"

His reply was in the affirmative.

"Well," I said, "I'll tell you what. My next book is also unwritten. And my unwritten book is exactly the same as A Writer of Very Successful Commercial Fiction's unwritten book. I know I have an agent and I'm not supposed to discuss business but I am willing to sell you *my* unwritten book for precisely the same price that you paid for A Writer of Very Successful Commercial Fiction's unwritten book."

My dinner companion declined courteously and then offered me, for my unwritten book, a sum in six figures.

"Call my agent," I replied, and turned to my right.

The next morning I was awakened by a telephone call from said agent, informing me that she had just received and rejected the offer of a sum in six figures for the movie rights to my unwritten book.

"I think we can get more," she said. "I'll talk to you later."

I mulled this over and called her back. "Look," I said, "last year I earned four thousand dollars for the things that I wrote. This year I've been offered two sums in six figures for the things that I have not written. Obviously I've been going about this whole business in the wrong way. Not writing, it turns out, is not only fun but also, it would appear, enormously profitable. Call that movie fellow and tell him that I have several unwritten books—maybe as many as twenty." I lit another cigarette, coughed deeply and accepted reality. "Well, at least ten, anyway. We'll clean up."

We chatted a bit more and I hung up reluctantly, being well aware of how important talking on the telephone was to my newly lucrative career of not writing. I forged ahead, though, and am pleased to report that by careful application and absolute imposition of will, I spent the entire day not writing a single word.

That evening I attended an exhibit of the work of a well-known artist. I inquired as to the prices of the attractively displayed pictures, stalwartly registered only mild surprise and spent the remainder of the evening filled with an uneasy greed.

The next day, immediately upon awakening, I telephoned my agent and announced that I wanted to diversify—become more visual. Not writing was fine for the acquisition of a little capital but the real money was, it seemed to me, in not painting. No longer was I going to allow myself to be confined to one form. I was now not going to work in two mediums.

I spent the next few days in happy contemplation of my impending wealth. While it was true that no actual checks were rolling in, I was not born yesterday and know that these things take time. Inspired by my discovery, I began to look at things in an entirely new light. One weekend while driving through the countryside, I was struck by the thought that among the things that I cultivate, land is not one of them.

First thing Monday morning, I called my agent. "Listen," I said, "I know this is a little outside your field, but I would appreciate it if you would contact the Department of Agriculture and notify them that I am presently, and have been for quite some time, not growing any wheat. I know that the acreage in my apartment is small, but let's see what we can get. And while you're at it, why don't you try the Welfare Department? I don't have a job, either. That ought to be worth a few bucks."

She said she'd see what she could do and hung up, leaving me to fend for myself.

I didn't paint—a piece of cake. I grew no wheat—a snap. I remained unemployed—nothing to it. And as for not writing, well, when it comes to not writing, I'm the real thing, the genuine article, an old pro. Except, I must admit, when it comes to a deadline. A deadline is really out of my hands. There are others to consider, obligations to be met. In the case of a deadline I almost invariably falter, and as you can see, this time was no exception. This piece was due. I did it. But as the more observant among you may note, I exercised at least a modicum of restraint. This piece is too short —much too short. Forgive me, but I needed the money. If you're going to do something, do it halfway. Business is business.